By
Faith
I
Live

BY FAITH I LIVE

WILLIAM A. FAGAL

SOUTHERN
PUBLISHING
ASSOCIATION,
NASHVILLE,
TENNESSEE

2/17²
/3

First printing, December, 1965,   100,000 copies
Second printing, January, 1966,   100,000 copies

PREFACE

When the woman of Samaria told the inhabitants of Sychar about her personal conversation with Jesus, leading to her acceptance of Him as the Messiah, they, too, believed. Though some may reason that there was nothing too unusual about this "chance meeting" by Jacob's well, the power of her own witness, with the blessing of Heaven, led souls to truth. Without doubt personal testimony regarding one's own experience with Christ has proved to be a most convincing argument. For this reason, this book is written in the first person.

This volume contains numerous personal references and experiences—probably none of them especially memorable or earth-shaking. However, simple though they are, out of them and many others has come the faith by which I live. I share them with exactly the same hope which inspired the woman of Samaria, that those who hear and read may be led to accept the Lord Jesus as their Saviour and may find a living, personal faith as satisfying and rewarding as my own.

Tested in the crucible of experience, my faith has proved to be both reasonable and attractive. Without its sustaining hope, life for me would be abysmally empty and dismally depressing at best. But with it I have an inner happiness and a confident hope for the here and now and for the days that are before us. May you find the same.

WILLIAM A. FAGAL

CONTENTS

GOD'S AMAZING BOOK

YOU ARE an American journalist. You have come to our country to spy on us and incite public opinion against us. Where do you intend to go in our country?"

Patiently I tried to explain to the immigration officer at the airport in Baghdad that I had come to his country to visit the site of old Babylon, the wonder of the ancient world, the city of antiquity which would correspond to our modern New York or London. But secretly I began to wish I had not been so brash as to attempt this visit.

"Babylon!" he exploded. "You expect me to believe that you, an intelligent man [I nodded acknowledgment of the compliment], have traveled halfway around the world just to see Babylon? There is nothing to see in Babylon. You must know that, and you must have some other purpose in coming here."

I told him exactly why I had come. I knew I would never be allowed into the country if I did not, and I knew also that I might even have some trouble immediately in getting out if I could not gain his confidence. Obviously he was in no mood to be trifled with. He wanted no spies in his politically sensitive country, teetering as it was at that time between East and West.

After a long period of discussion, he seemed to believe my story and stamped my passport, granting me the coveted entrance.

Babylon, I felt, was worth a few risks and hazards because of its place in Bible prophecy. This city was one of a number about which very specific details were recorded in advance. These prophecies, entirely contrary to what anyone might have guessed or supposed at the time, were fulfilled to the letter.

As far as I am concerned, confidence in the Bible's prophecies regarding the future is provided by the exactness of the fulfillment of its prophecies regarding the past. And, incidentally, any book containing absolutely fulfilled prophecies would necessarily have to be a different sort of book from the ordinary. In fact, I am convinced that it would have to be inspired, for no one but God can look ahead for a single moment and with complete fidelity indicate exactly what the future holds. He claims this ability for Himself and cites it as proof of His unique position in the universe. Here is what He says: "I am God, and there is none like me, declaring the end from the beginning, and from ancient times the things that are not yet done." Isaiah 46:9, 10. "Have not I told thee from that time, and have declared it? ye are even my witnesses." Isaiah 44:8.

Two prophets, Isaiah and Jeremiah, were moved to make exceedingly dire predictions about Babylon at the time when it was the wonder and pride of the ancient world. It had been growing steadily in power and prestige, and there was absolutely no reason to suspect that the future would be any different from the past. This beautiful city was renowned for its hanging gardens, its towering walls, its lofty palaces and ornate temples. Babylon's location was unexcelled, reposing as it did in the midst of the most fertile region then known to man.

And Babylon's contributions intellectually had measured up remarkably to her opportunities. Her men of learning had invented an alphabet, worked out problems in mathematics, attained a high perfection of skill in the making of textile fabrics, studied successfully the motions of the heavenly bodies, and elaborated a system of law. In almost any branch of science that you could name, Babylon had made a beginning. Much of the art and learning of Greece which attracted the world's attention in later years had its origin in Babylon.

But when Babylon was at the zenith of her power and prestige, here is what the Bible prophets dared to say and write about her future:

"And Babylon, the glory of kingdoms, the beauty of the Chaldees' excellency, shall be as when God overthrew Sodom and Gomorrah. It shall never be inhabited, neither shall it be dwelt in from generation to generation: neither shall the Arabian pitch tent there; neither shall the shepherds make their fold there. But wild beasts of the desert shall lie there; and their houses shall be full of doleful creatures." Isaiah 13:19-21.

"And Babylon shall become heaps, a dwellingplace for dragons, an astonishment, and an hissing, without an inhabitant." "The broad walls of Babylon shall be utterly broken, and her high gates shall be burned with fire." Jeremiah 51:37, 58.

This is why I wanted to visit the site of Babylon—to see for myself how these daring Bible prophecies were tragically, even catastrophically, fulfilled. I knew what to expect, but as I approached what was once proud Babylon, I could be more sympathetic with the immigration officer who refused to believe that I had come to his country merely to see this. Truly, nothing much is left to see—except exactly what the prophet saw in vision hundreds of years ago and recorded unerringly.

Of this city ruling the ancient world God had said that not a single inhabitant would survive. And yet He indicated that a small nomadic people, the Arabs, who at that time had none of the culture, achievements, or permanence of the Babylonians, would live on. Have you ever seen a Babylonian? Neither have I. As far as I know, not a single one is left. And yet the prophecy indicated that the Arabs would continue on indefinitely, for "neither shall the Arabian pitch tent there." And the Arabs are widespread—except that none live in Babylon.

For a time after these prophecies of doom had been written, it appeared that just the opposite would take place. One hundred years later the city had assumed new importance and grandeur. Nebuchadnezzar, its new monarch, launched a successful program of building up the city and thus adding to its prestige.

Had a scoffer cared to, he might have held up the prophecies to very real and difficult-to-answer ridicule. Men might have laughed at God and His Word, saying, "A century has passed—a century of progress—'an astonishment' indeed! And the future will be better than the past. The Bible is a false book." They might even have added to their ridicule by giving a definition of the Bible similar to this one published by the Soviet Publishing House in Moscow: "The Bible is a collection of fantastic legends without scientific support. It is full of historical mistakes and contradictions. It serves as a factor for gaining power and subjugating the unknowing nations."

But Babylon today is indeed "heaps." I found it to be "an astonishment" and "without an inhabitant," full only of the "wild beasts of the desert"—not even a stop on the railroad anymore. As we approached the great area covered by this once-mighty city, I would never have recognized it for what it was had I not been in the company of others who had been there before.

We parked the car next to one of the huge mounds, or "heaps," and climbed up into what had been the summer palace of Nebuchadnezzar. Little was left to indicate its former glory. Bricks bearing the name of the former monarch who reigned here lay all about our feet, verifying that we were at the right place. But not even enough bricks were left standing to recognize that this had once been a building.

Down the road a bit farther, other "heaps" revealed the location of the original city itself. A light rain began to fall upon us, adding to the desolation of the scene. At length we stood at the very place where Belshazzar had conducted his celebrated feast the night the handwriting of God traced upon the wall the words, "Thou art weighed in the balances, and art found wanting." That night Babylon fell to the invading armies of the Medes and Persians.

As I contemplated the scene, a wild jackal jumped down into his lair on the very place where the priceless treasures and riches of antiquity had once been displayed. For some reason I shuddered in the damp cold.

As I surveyed all this, I silently repeated to myself some of the inspired words of Jeremiah and Isaiah about this once-proud city. No doubt beset my mind that day—in Babylon I saw Bible prophecy vindicated. A new certainty came upon me that the Bible is indeed a true Book. The Bible contains hundreds of prophecies, and all of them have been fulfilled as accurately and specifically as have the ones about Babylon.

A few days later on the coast of the Mediterranean Sea I visited two cities thirty miles apart—Tyre and Sidon—about which Bible prophecy has spoken. Sidon had been declining for centuries, and it was taken and destroyed in 351 b.c. by Artaxerxes Ochus, the king of Persia. It would seem that it would surely soon be gone entirely after that. But though the prophet in Ezekiel 28:20-23 prophesied trouble for it, he did not prophesy extinction. I thought of that as I drove into little Sidon, still inhabited until this day, despite its long and bloody history.

But Bible prophecy had indicated something quite different for Tyre, the major port city of the Phoenicians, the famed builders of ships. Tyre was mistress of the seas, just as Babylon was of the land. But this is what Ezekiel prophesied for her:

"And they shall destroy the walls of Tyrus, and break down her towers: I will also scrape her dust from her, and make her like the top of a rock." "They shall lay thy stones and thy timber and thy dust in the midst of the water." "And I will make thee like the top of a rock: thou shalt be a place to spread nets upon; thou shalt be built no more: for I the Lord have spoken it, saith the Lord God." "Though thou be sought for, yet shalt thou never be found again, saith the Lord God." Ezekiel 26:4, 12, 14, 21.

This foretelling of destruction was as incredible as the prophecy regarding Babylon had been, and actually the people of Babylon were the ones who began the destruction of Tyre. Very shortly after Ezekiel's prediction Nebuchadnezzar began a long siege of Tyre, which lasted about twelve years. Tyre's inhabitants all fled to an offshore island when the city finally fell, and the conquerors destroyed it completely. But more was yet to be fulfilled, and it was accomplished in a most unusual way.

During the next 240 years Tyre existed on this island with the ruins of the ancient city plainly visible on the mainland. Then in 333 B.C. the new Tyre refused to bow to Alexander and was besieged. Since without ships Alexander could not reach the people on the island, he built a causeway to it, about 65 yards wide and 650 yards long.

In order to secure material for this ambitious project, he took all the ruins of the ancient city and cast them into the water, just as the prophecy had foretold. As he searched for additional materials, he even scraped the dirt and dust off the top of the rocks and threw them into the water as well. When finally the causeway was completed, the new city of Tyre was no longer on an island, but rather was at the end of a peninsula. The city was then taken easily by Alexander.

Because all the building material has been scraped into the ocean, archaeologists cannot find the spot where that ancient city stood. What an amazing fulfillment of the prophecy, "Though thou be sought for, yet shalt thou never be found again, saith the Lord God." Pillars and stones used to build the causeway are still visible at the water's edge. As I walked on this causeway and looked down at these relics in the water and searched in vain for the ancient Tyre, I again saw Bible prophecy vindicated —to the letter.

The Bible is a Book in which we can have confidence. Only those who have never had opportunity to check the accuracy of its claims could doubt its veracity. The more one knows and learns, the more he can believe in this Book. True faith is necessary as well; but so much can be proved about its claims, so much is known, that anyone who really wants to believe should have no difficulty in accepting the unknown.

This Book declares itself to be inspired of God. "All scripture is given by inspiration of God, and is profitable for doctrine, for reproof, for correction, for instruction in righteousness." 2 Timothy 3:16. "For the prophecy came not in old time by the will of man: but holy men of God spake as they were moved by the Holy Ghost." 2 Peter 1:21.

The Bible claims itself to be written by men who were God-inspired. This is just what I believe it to be. I have seen its prophecies vindicated, not just the few mentioned here, but hundreds of others which could have been cited. I know that a power greater than man has had to be behind it. As far as I am concerned, that power is God.

Do you have confidence in this Book which is the Book of books? Have you read its sacred pages? Have you let its message speak to your own heart? You will be a different man or woman if you do. Start today.

GOD'S AMAZING GIFT

AT HIGH NOON in Cairo, Egypt, I stood just about in the middle of a long bridge spanning the Nile. The bright warm sunshine and the joy of my first visit to these unusual surroundings conspired to make me especially glad to be alive.

So fascinated was I by the commercial sailboats with their native crews attired in Egyptian dress passing on the waters beneath me that I failed to hear some signal given for all pedestrians to leave the bridge. Only when I heard a piercing siren did I look up from the river and discover to my consternation that I was the only individual remaining on the long span.

Feeling most conspicuous, I gave quick consideration to and rejection of the idea of diving into the Nile and swimming for shore. Additional unworkable plans died at birth. With something akin to horror I watched the rapid approach of several official-looking black cars preceded by policemen on motorcycles. The motorcade rushed headlong toward me, apparently to place me under arrest for my little-understood crime. I envisioned myself spending a long time in a gloomy prison cell far from home.

But when the accelerating vehicles reached me, they sped on by without even hesitating, and I watched with relief as they rounded the corner and disappeared. And what had it all been about? Gamal Abdel Nasser, Egypt's president, had just gone home for lunch!

As the bridge traffic moved about me once more and my heart settled down to its normal pace, I concluded that it is rather nice to be on top—a president, a prime minister, or anything relatively similar.

I have observed many times how difficult it is for an individual to step down from a high position of influence. And although my station in life is not exactly high, I would find it exceedingly difficult to step down very far, even from what I enjoy.

In some lands I have visited poverty is extreme. I have seen little mud huts which must serve as homes for large families. The little dwellings are so inadequate that all the family cannot get inside at once, but it is all they can afford. I have seen the grass mats on which such individuals must sleep on the ground out under the stars. Since there are not enough grass mats to go around, several must sleep on them at once the wide way with feet extending off the sides and with no cover to keep them warm. My heart has gone out to these unfortunate people, but I have never found myself willing to give up my comfortable bed and warm home in order to live as they do.

But when our Lord Jesus Christ left heaven and came here to live among us, He left a sinless, perfect place and came to live with us amid our sin and imperfection. He exchanged the adoration of angels for the company of men who spit upon Him, reviled Him, cursed Him, and ultimately crucified Him. Why did He do it? There is only one answer. Love! Love for us who did not know Him and who apparently could not care less.

Who was this Jesus in whom "born-again Christians" have so much confidence? References to Him run like a golden thread throughout the entire Bible. All history becomes in fact "His story" when we know Him, for we can look nowhere without seeing Him.

Saul of Tarsus became one of Christ's most ardent disciples, even though like us he never saw Him in the flesh. With divinely illumined understanding he wrote comprehensively and preached forcefully about the Saviour. Known as the Apostle Paul following his conversion, he wrote these words to a group of believers in the city of Philippi: "Let this mind be in you, which was also in Christ Jesus: who, being in the form of God, thought it not robbery to be equal with God: but made himself of no reputation, and took upon him the form of a servant, and was made in the likeness of men: and being found in fashion as a man, he humbled himself, and became obedient unto death, even the death of the cross." Philippians 2:5-8.

Paul asserted that Jesus originally was "in the form of God." This is exactly what the Bible elsewhere teaches. Referring to Christ as "the Word," the prophet John says, "In the beginning was the Word, and the Word was with God, and the Word was God." John 1:1. Without doubt then, Jesus existed in the very beginning along with God the Father and on an equality with Him. He, too, was called God. But He willingly gave up His position, condescending to come to this earth because of the human family's need, which only He could meet.

Consequently Paul in awe gently explains that He "made himself of no reputation, and took upon him the form of a servant, and was made in the likeness of men: and being found in fashion as a man, he humbled himself." Here is a most amazing thought. Christ voluntarily stepped down from the highest position of the universe in order that He might lift us up.

It is not easy for a person to step down. Life is much happier as one moves up in position, influence, and prestige. Only exceedingly strong motivation could influence anyone to willingly reverse the normally sought direction. But Christ stepped *down!*

Many years ago when the first Christian missionaries went to Japan, one of them was requested to teach English to a young Japanese. The lessons began, and after a time the youth was set to work translating the Gospel of John as a helpful exercise.

After a while the student, restless and agitated, blurted out the question, "Who is this man about whom I have been reading, this Jesus? You call Him a man, but He must be God." This same conclusion has been reached by many others. It is not unwarranted.

Admittedly some see little in Jesus of Nazareth. To them He is simply another man, a good man, to be sure, but a man nonetheless. They volunteer sympathetically that it was too bad He suffered martyrdom at such an early age, only thirty-three, and speculate on what He might have accomplished had He lived longer. But we who believe Him to be the Lord Jesus Christ, God's own Son, engage in no such idle speculation. We believe that He as the Messiah accomplished on Calvary's cross exactly what He came to this world to accomplish—the salvation of the human race from sin.

Some who question our conclusions will be quick to point out that the people who lived in Christ's time saw nothing unusual in Him. Jesus once asked the Pharisees, "What think ye of Christ? whose son is he?" Matthew 22:42. Priests, Pharisees, and national leaders rejected completely His claim to being the Christ, giving no credence to the idea that He was the long-awaited, divinely promised Messiah.

The people of His own time noticed little which was striking or commanding in His appearance. But such overlooked a significant prophecy regarding this very aspect of the coming Messiah: "He hath no form nor comeliness; and when we shall see him, there is no beauty that we should desire him. He is despised and rejected of men." Isaiah 53:2, 3. In Christ every prophecy recorded in the Old Testament regarding the Messiah, even this one, was fulfilled.

In attempting to judge an individual only by appearances, many disastrous mistakes have been made. The great musician Mozart was engaged to a young lady who later became unhappy with her choice and broke off their engagement. But when the world began to recognize Mozart's greatness, she commented upon her refusal of him by referring to his smallness of stature: "I knew nothing of the greatness of his genius. I saw only a little man."

Just so, some in Christ's time saw nothing of what He really was, for they were expecting a dashing military hero, perhaps even a swaggering, boastful despot who would decisively free Israel from national servitude to Rome. In looking for one who would exchange Israel's satellite position for a stellar role in the affairs of men, they overlooked completely the Servant of servants, the Son of God, who came to save mankind all right, but from sin in general rather than from Rome in particular.

Many people have stumbled over some Bible claims for Christ. A Christian and a non-Christian were conversing one day about the virgin birth of Jesus. The non-Christian, calculating to settle the question once and for all, asked, "If I should tell you that a child had been born in this city without a father, would you believe it?" The Christian's thoughtful and wise reply was, "Yes, if he were to live as Jesus lived."

The life of Christ on this earth proved beyond all doubt that He was different from any other being who ever lived among men. Doubters like Thomas were forced to exclaim, "My Lord and my God." A centurion who had watched His closing hours felt circumstances wring from him the startling confession, "Truly this man was the Son of God." A proud Pharisee ruler, protecting his reputation by seeking Jesus out under cover of darkness, confessed, "Rabbi, we know that thou art a teacher come from God: for no man can do these miracles that thou doest, except God be with him." John 3:2. To this we who believe in Him, gladly confessing Him as our Saviour and Lord, can agree without mental reservation.

Christ loved us and God loved us. "For God so loved the world, that he gave his only begotten Son, that whosoever believeth in him should not perish, but have everlasting life." John 3:16. Jesus did not come to this world to rule over us as a king. He "made himself of no reputation." He "took upon him the form of a servant." He "humbled himself," and ultimately He even "became obedient unto death." Imagine it—*God* willing to undergo even *death* in order that He might save us! And what is more, His was not an easy, serene, beautiful death. Even here He plumbed the depths for us by accepting "even the death of the cross."

The Romans practiced crucifixion when Christ lived on this earth, but they did so according to certain well-defined rules. They would never crucify another Roman, for a death as horrible as this must not be inflicted upon one of their own. They reserved death by crucifixion as a method of punishing their slaves and the vilest of their criminals.

Can you imagine what a disadvantage it must have been to the early Christians to bear to the world the message that their Jesus, whom they confidently accepted as the long-awaited Messiah, had been *crucified* as a despised slave or a common criminal? Those who might have been tempted to believe in Him would certainly be deterred when they learned of His ignominious death. Already handicapped by their misconception of the Messiah's mission, many would erroneously conclude that if this Man had truly been God's own Son, God never would have allowed Him to die on a cross. Do you see what a temptation it would have been to the early Christians to hide the place of the cross in His experience?

But the early Christians did not try to obscure the manner of His death. Paul stated boldly, even proudly, "We preach Christ crucified, unto the Jews a stumblingblock [and I am sure it must have been], and unto the Greeks foolishness; but unto them which are called, both Jews and Greeks, Christ the power of God, and the wisdom of God." 1 Corinthians 1:23, 24. You see, Paul had come to understand that Jesus voluntarily had gone through all of this for *us*. Therefore while the crucified Christ might be a stumbling block to some and foolishness to others, the cross had come to represent to Paul the power of the Almighty, demonstrating what divinity would do to save mankind.

And so it is that we, the Christian believers of today, preach Christ crucified, proud and eternally grateful for the fact that He willingly accepted the most awful death of all in order to effect our salvation.

Paul states authoritatively, "Every tongue should confess that Jesus Christ is Lord, to the glory of God the Father." Philippians 2:11. We should indeed. And what a privilege it is to confess Jesus Christ as Lord. How proud I am to be able to bear His name, calling myself a Christian. How undeserving I am of His love and sacrifice.

He did not need to atone on Calvary for any guilt of His own. Rather it was I and you and all the rest of the human family who have sinned. We are the ones who should have had to die for our wrongdoing. But "for our sake he made him to be sin who knew no sin, so that in him we might become the righteousness of God." (2 Corinthians 5:21, R.S.V.)

What do you think of Jesus Christ? Have you confessed Him as your Lord? That question has been asked of a great many people with a variety of answers. The Pharisees with scorn replied, "He eateth . . . with publicans and sinners." The high priest, Caiaphas, spat out the words, "He is a blasphemer because he said, 'Hereafter shall ye see the Son of man sitting on the right hand of power, and coming in the clouds of heaven.'"

But Pilate's opinion was, "I find no fault in this man." And Judas, His betrayer who sold Him for thirty pieces of silver, testified, "I have sinned in that I have betrayed the innocent blood." John the Baptist exclaimed, "Behold the Lamb of God." Peter affirmed to his Master, "Thou art the Christ, the Son of the living God." Paul, who had persecuted Christ's followers, testified, "I count all things but loss for the excellency of the knowledge of Christ Jesus my Lord." The angels of heaven sang forth, "Unto you is born . . . a Saviour, which is Christ the Lord." And God in heaven, the Father of us all, confirmed our faith in the words, "This is my beloved Son, in whom I am well pleased."

What appeared to be a large stone lay for centuries in a shallow brook in North Carolina. Those who happened to pass by, if they noticed it at all, saw it only as an ugly dark lump and left it undisturbed. But a poor farmer, deciding that it would be just the thing needed to hold his door ajar, took it home and used it for that purpose. A geologist, accidentally stopping by his home one day, examined the stone and recognized it as something more. It turned out to be the biggest lump of gold ever found east of the Rockies. And then everyone wondered how so many people could have looked upon it and yet failed to see what it really was.

The sad truth is that many people have looked upon Jesus with the same unseeing eyes. Some saw in Him only another Galilean, and they continued on their way. Others saw in Him a Prophet, and listening to His gracious words they were blessed. Only a few recognized Him as the Messiah, but they gladly devoted their lives to Him.

Some today see in Jesus only a wonderful example of what all of us ought to be. But others of us see in Him "the Lamb of God, which taketh away the sin of the world." We know that His blood can cleanse us from past sins and that He can give us power to live victoriously in the future. As the result, we have accepted Him as our Saviour and Lord. We have experienced His power to transform a human life, and we are glad.

"Every tongue should confess that Jesus Christ is Lord, to the glory of God the Father." Philippians 2:11. I gladly do so. Do you?

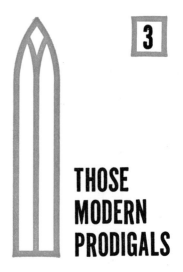

THOSE
MODERN
PRODIGALS

WELL PAST midnight on a cold morning in January I was driving alone through northern Tennessee. Perhaps my depleted energy may be blamed for my poor judgment (never more than mediocre at best), for I did what I now recognize to be a very foolish thing.

My bobbing headlights suddenly illuminated a slender and obviously very cold hitchhiker. In an instant of shallow thinking, I reasoned that I needed him to keep me awake and he needed me to bring him closer to his destination. After an impulsive, tire-squealing stop, my shivering passenger in his early twenties and I were on our way again with the car's heater turned up to the full to thaw him out.

We made small talk for a while. How far was I going? About fifty miles down the road to a city where I hoped to spend the remainder of the night. Where was he headed? His hometown about five hundred miles away. Where had he started from? The other side of the United States. He had been on the road for several days.

As we traveled swiftly on in the night and more of his story slowly unfolded, I had cause to fear that picking him up had been very brash indeed. He had left home to work for a traveling road company, had concluded that he was being underpaid, and had finally resorted to armed robbery of his employer to settle the score. A brief period of crime followed, culminating in a comparatively short prison sentence. Freed and living in a dismal furnished room, he had found it almost impossible to get re-established in any kind of regular gainful employment and had succumbed to almost complete discouragement just before starting on this trip.

About this time I began to wonder about his present state of mind. Might he have a gun in his bulging pocket right now, and momentarily might he decide that my automobile and the cash in my pocket were exactly what he needed to end his streak of "bad luck"? I stifled an impulse to bring the car to a halt and attempt some ruse to discharge my now feared passenger. Perhaps the fact that I could not think of a plausible excuse really made the decision for me, and we rode on together.

He never asked me who or what I was, and for some reason I did not volunteer the information. But slowly I came to see him as a young man very much in need of help. I told myself that this very night might well be a time of far-reaching decision in his heretofore unfortunate life. Suppressing my fears, I deliberately set about to encourage him to make right choices in his life from now on.

He had telephoned his widowed mother collect before starting out and had heard her joyfully reassure him of her love as she urged him to return home. He had started out immediately, though almost completely without funds. As the result, he had not eaten a decent meal in several days. He had spent the last night sleeping in a barn by the side of the road. His clothes were unpressed, and he badly needed a haircut.

After his story had been told, I cautiously suggested the advisability of attempting to forget the past as he pressed on hopefully toward an entirely different kind of future. Admittedly life in the "far country" had not been good, and he had chosen to react to his misfortune in the wrong way; but he never need make the same mistakes again. I spoke confidently of the fact, very real to me, that God would forgive him for all that was behind him, and like the prodigal of Jesus' parable, he could return to the welcome of parental love and fully restored sonship.

I warmed to my subject as I felt that he was grasping and accepting my sincerely offered encouragements. My personal fears were all but forgotten and replaced instead with a growing feeling of gratitude for what I concluded had been a divine Providence that had placed this homeward-bound boy beside me in the night.

As we approached the city which would be the point where our routes would separate, I made a suggestion. I would be staying at a hotel for the night, and if he would permit me to do so, I would be glad to secure a room for him. He agreed; and after getting settled, I took him to a nearby lunch counter and secured a meal for him. Before retiring, I gave him money to be used the next day for a haircut and for more food. His last words to me before we separated were, "This is a small world, and someday I may well meet you again. I'll never forget your kindness to me tonight." His appreciation sweetened my sleep that night and made my homeward journey the next day happy.

Pensive and penitent prodigals—this world has seen many of them. But have you ever thought that in a wider sense all of us are prodigals? Like the original prodigal son of old, we have all wandered from home and sought the pleasures of sin in the far country. The undeniable truth of the matter as concisely stated in the Bible is that "all have sinned, and come short of the glory of God." "There is none righteous, no, not one." "All our righteousnesses are as filthy rags." But many of us know from experience the undying love of a heavenly Father, who, when we call Him collect from that far country, reassures us of His love and urges us to come home.

In a certain town in Pennsylvania lived a young man who, becoming bored with farm life, left for the big city, where he plunged unrestrained into a pretty sordid life. Although never hearing from him, his parents did not cease to pray that God would bring him to his senses. After a time—too long a time—when the emptiness of his new life began to descend full force upon him, he wondered if he would possibly be welcome were he to return home.

In a momentary burst of courage he started out, but upon his arrival at his hometown he was so ashamed of his appearance and his past that he reboarded the train and went on a station or two farther. There from a cheap hotel next to the railroad station he wrote a letter home, telling of his remorse and requesting assurance of his parents' forgiveness. The next day he would visit his hometown; and if his parents would receive him back, he asked that they hang a sheet on the clothesline as a sign. What did that mother do? She took all the sheets in the house and hung them all out to show the abundance of her pardon.

And that in a limited way is an example of God's attitude toward all of us. The "good news" of the gospel is that His love knows no limit and His forgiveness encompasses anyone who wants to be forgiven. He has sent Jesus, His only Son, to this world that we might see that there are no limits to how far He will go to save us. Calvary's cross provides the way back, the bridge between earth and heaven which spans the gulf between all of us prodigals and our heavenly Father. "Though your sins be as scarlet, they shall be as white as snow; though they be red like crimson, they shall be as wool." Isaiah 1:18.

Of Jesus it had been said, "Behold, a virgin shall be with child, and shall bring forth a son, and they shall call his name Emmanuel, which being interpreted is, God with us." Matthew 1:23. Jesus was in reality God in human flesh come down to save us. As a member of the Trinity, He was God the Son; and He became our Saviour. He was a new kind of God, one totally unfamiliar to the world's concepts. Remember that the God of the Jews of the Old Testament was thought of as being so holy that they did not even dare pronounce His name. Whenever they came to the name "Jahweh," the name for God in the Old Testament, they would cease reading aloud and in a hushed and awed tone say only, "The name." Because they never spoke the name aloud, they even forgot how to pronounce it. Rather than being considered close to them and concerned with their problems, God was thought to be rather austere, far off and unapproachable.

At other periods men have thought of God as living somewhere out in outer space, and therefore utterly detached and disinterested in human affairs.

But in Christ men received the concept of a God so interested in human affairs that He willingly came down to live among us, sharing in all our experiences. He was truly "Emmanuel, . . . God with us."

After Jesus Christ had lived among men, it could never be said that God did not understand all about us and our problems or that He did not care. In Christ, God had been here too, and the experience brought the certainty that He fully understands everything through which we pass. He knows all about human weakness and how strong is the temptation to evil. He knows how often we succumb, and He knows our remorse and guilt. He knows how bad we really are. And the wonder of it all is that despite this, He loves us supremely and wants to save us.

Do you see yourself as needing something which you do not now possess? Are you therefore dissatisfied with your accomplishments? Sir James Simpson made a number of scientific discoveries, including that of the anesthetic property of chloroform. He became world renowned as the result. Near the close of his life a young student asked him what he considered to be his greatest discovery. His thoughtful reply was, "The greatest discovery I ever made was that I am a great sinner but that Jesus Christ is my Saviour." I am convinced that this is the greatest discovery which could be made by any man.

What a marvelous discovery it is to find that One loved us, even *you* and even *me*, enough to pay the penalty for our sins on the cross! Let these inspired words reach you: "Who his own self bare our sins in his own body on the tree, that we, being dead to sins, should live unto righteousness: by whose stripes ye were healed." 1 Peter 2:24.

Some feel that they are hampered in faith by theological considerations and intellectual doubts. While it is conceivable that these things may be obstructing the faith of some, yet it is easy to use this as an excuse.

A certain New York lawyer several years ago stated that he would be a Christian if he could really have it proved to him that Jesus rose from the dead. A clergyman friend said, "I will be glad to give you what I feel is conclusive evidence of this fact." And he later submitted to him a manuscript containing convincing factual arguments on the subject.

A week later as the lawyer returned the manuscript, he stated, "I must say that I believe now beyond all reasonable doubts from the historical evidence of credible witnesses that Jesus Christ rose from the dead." Then he added significantly, "But I am no more a Christian now than I was when I took the evidence from you a week ago." Speaking in a lower tone he said, "I have found out that my chief trouble is not with my head, but with my heart."

And really, is this not the chief trouble of most individuals? It is sin which blinds and separates. It is sin which closes the mind and the heart to eternal truths. But Jesus has provided the answer to the sin problem. He can give a man a new heart and change him so much that he can truly be called "born again." Born again! What a hopeful and challenging promise!

As a matter of fact, this spiritual rebirth is considered by Jesus to be an absolute essential in every man's life. To the inquiring Nicodemus, a ruler of the Jews, He said categorically, "Except a man be born again, he cannot see the kingdom of God." John 3:3.

A man who crossed the Valley of Dead Men in the South Sea Islands reached a little shelter at its end. Looking back, he saw his tracks in the sand and noticed how crooked his path had been, even though he had intended to walk straight. Introspectively he exclaimed, "That is the story of my life. Every footprint and pathway crooked." Hours later, however, as he looked again for his tracks, no marks were left. Every footprint was gone, for in the interim the tide had been in and receded, leaving no sign of the crooked path.

This is exactly what Jesus does for our unhappy past if we allow Him. He has promised, "I have blotted out, as a thick cloud, thy transgressions, and, as a cloud, thy sins." Isaiah 44:22. His blood shed on Calvary like a tranquil tide washes away every stain of sin in our lives and removes every evidence of our transgression.

No one really enjoys being told that he has made a mistake or has sinned. A young lady who makes no profession of spiritual things today told me recently that the unpleasant memory she retains of her childhood church was of a minister thundering, "You have sinned," as he pointed a long bony finger down from his pulpit seemingly at her. The truth is that probably very few of us need the finger-pointing or the thunderings, for our own consciences do both most adequately. As the result, our self-respect is threadbare and our self-disappointment keen.

Marcus Whitman, a pioneer missionary to the Pacific Northwest, preached to the Indians there of the cross of Jesus with all of its implications for holier living. They would often protest his sermons and ask him to give them instead "good talk." They begged, "Tell us that we are good men, brave men." We smile at simple men's desire for approbation whether or not it is deserved, and perhaps we fail to recognize that some of the simple clings to all of us. But will men be helped by ignoring the problems common to all and concentrating on "good talk"? Of course not.

The simple truth with redemptive power is that we are all sinners, but in Jesus Christ we have a great and loving Saviour who wants to free us from our past misdeeds and give us the ability to live daily as we ought.

We should not hesitate to come to Him because we recognize our unworthiness. We should come rather as we see our need, and He with the love of the prodigal's father welcomes us back, washes away the record of our past with the tide of His own blood, and sends us on our way renewed, restored, and remade.

A young woman, anxious about her own spiritual condition, picked up from the pavement a page from a hymnal containing this stanza:

> "Let not conscience make you linger,
> Nor of fitness fondly dream;
> All the fitness He requireth
> Is to feel your need of Him."

The words drove her to her knees in prayer. After she had poured out her heart and asked forgiveness for her sins, she arose with the inner assurance that God had accepted her. The same thing can happen for you, too, if you accept the Lord Jesus Christ as your Saviour and confess your sins to Him.

"If thou shalt confess with thy mouth the Lord Jesus, and shalt believe in thine heart that God hath raised him from the dead, thou shalt be saved." Romans 10:9. Will you accept Him as your Saviour? Right now?

GOD'S ROLE IN SUFFERING

I DON'T SEE how there could be a God in heaven who would allow my mother to suffer so much," the grief-stricken girl in her late teens sobbed. We were driving along behind a black, shiny hearse on what was to me a too-familiar route to the cemetery.

She was right. Her mother had suffered a great deal. I knew it as well as she. I remember well the day that her mother came into my study in the church and I met her for the first time, a frail and pale woman of about thirty-five. It was evident that she had at one time been beautiful, but it was also apparent that illness had taken a heavy toll. She had begun the conversation by telling me that she had recently been informed that she was afflicted with inoperable cancer and that she could not expect to live much longer.

Thoughtfully she told me that she had been brought up in a Christian home, one of my own faith, but had wandered far away from God. In the intervening years she had, in her words, "made a perfect mess" of her life. She had married very young, and two of her three marriages had ended unhappily in divorce. Her present husband had turned out to be a confirmed alcoholic.

She then stated simply her feeling that she could face the future without fear if only once again she could get her life completely right with God.

We talked on several occasions about it and prayed together. She rededicated her heart and life fully to the Lord Jesus, and I was happy one day to baptize her and make her a part of the church again. It did something for my own heart to see the radiant Christian experience which quickly blossomed from what had been the hard soil of her heart.

A few weeks later the ravages of her disease made her bedfast. She did indeed suffer greatly, yet even through her pain shone the renewed beauty of her radiant life. She was very brave, perhaps even heroic, through the period which followed, and her faith in God's goodness never seemed to waver for a moment.

But now it was all over. In her preconversion lifetime she had alienated most of her friends, and they had not had opportunity in the last weeks of her life to discover that God had made her over. It had taken many hours of activity on my part to save her from a pauper's grave. Only her two teen-age daughters, her troubled and bewildered husband, and I were at the funeral. Only the daughters and I followed her to the grave.

As her daughter looked back on the entire experience, she wondered why a good God had allowed it. I could only gently suggest that perhaps He had allowed it to save her—perhaps to save her loved ones.

Isaiah revealed, "In the year that king Uzziah died I saw also the Lord." Isaiah 6:1. Many have seen the Lord similarly through tragic loss and tears. In this way God keeps His promise that "all things work together for good to them that love God." (Romans 8:28.)

Many people have questioned God's goodness similarly when confronted with comparable situations. It is hard to see a loved one suffer. Ofttimes during such a period one wonders why it has to be. There are no quick and easy answers to the complex problems of life, but there are some things which will help us better to understand. Patiently I tried to explain them to the sorrowing daughters that day.

In the first place, it is important for us to know and ever to remember that God did not create suffering. He never willed that we should know anything about it. Jesus carefully explained this in a parable found in Matthew 13:24-30, where He compared this world to a field in which a certain man sowed good seed. But that very night his enemy sowed weeds in the same soil. Later when all the seeds sprouted, the weeds became apparent among the wheat, and the servants could not understand where they had come from. They questioned the householder's seed, in effect blaming him for the apparent catastrophe. But his significant reply was, "An enemy hath done this."

This parable of our Lord describes what has happened to our world. As it came from the hand of the Creator, it was perfect, for the householder—God—had sowed only good seed. But one who does not love God—an enemy—managed soon afterward to sow an amazing number of weeds in our world, deliberately attempting to thwart God's eternal purposes. The evil with which we have to deal each day has come from this source. Who is this enemy? Where did he come from? Why does he hate God? And why does not God destroy him?

The Bible tells us that this enemy actually originated in heaven and that he was cast out because he chose paths of wrongdoing. "And there was war in heaven. . . . And the great dragon was cast out, that old serpent, called the Devil, and Satan, which deceiveth the whole world: he was cast out into the earth, and his angels were cast out with him." Revelation 12:7-9. Here the enemy is defined, and he is called the devil, and Satan. In Isaiah 14:12 he is referred to as Lucifer, which probably was his original name.

How did Lucifer come into being in the first place? God created him. But God did not create him a devil. The Scriptures say of him, "Thou wast perfect in thy ways from the day that thou wast created, till iniquity was found in thee." Ezekiel 28:15.

God, then, created him perfect. Lucifer himself chose the path of sin and made of himself a devil. The prophet Ezekiel speaks these words to him under the symbolic name of the king of Tyrus:

"Son of man, take up a lamentation upon the king of Tyrus, and say unto him, Thus saith the Lord God; Thou sealest up the sum, full of wisdom, and perfect in beauty. Thou hast been in Eden the garden of God; every precious stone was thy covering: . . . the workmanship of thy tabrets and of thy pipes was prepared in thee in the day that thou wast created. Thou art the anointed cherub that covereth; and I have set thee so: thou wast upon the holy mountain of God; thou hast walked up and down in the midst of the stones of fire." Ezekiel 28:12-14.

Satan was once a highly exalted angel. Before his fall from prominence and heaven he was both wise and beautiful. In fact, he was *full* of wisdom and *perfect* in beauty. The references to his tabrets and pipes would seem to indicate unexcelled musical ability. It is probable, therefore, that he might even have been the one who led the angelic hosts and choirs in song.

Besides this, he is referred to as "the anointed cherub that covereth," an expression referring to the ark of the covenant, where cherubim overshadowed "the mercy seat," God's throne. It could well have been, therefore, that this being stood next to God Himself, overshadowing the throne in heaven. It seems logical to conclude, therefore, that he may even have been the prime minister of God's heavenly government, second only in command to the Deity itself.

What, then, led to his fall? An unholy ambition took possession of this favored being. He wanted a higher place. It was just as simple as that. In his heart he said, "I will ascend. . . . I will exalt my throne. . . . I will be like the most High." Isaiah 14:13, 14. With all his advantages he still was not satisfied; he coveted the highest position. Envious of the Lord Jesus Christ, he wanted to be like the Most High Himself. How did he go about securing his own ends? He schemed, plotted, and finally settled on a plan.

First he laid claim to greater wisdom than God, implying that he would make a better ruler of the universe than Jehovah. He was proud of his talents and wisdom and felt himself capable of even greater responsibility. To him Ezekiel said, "Thine heart was lifted up because of thy beauty, thou hast corrupted thy wisdom by reason of thy brightness." Ezekiel 28:17. Finally, incomprehensible as it may seem, surrounded with all of the perfection and beauty of heaven itself, to this ambitious being it was said, "Thou hast sinned." Verse 16.

His sin finally took the form of open rebellion against God. He sowed discontent among the angels, saying something like this: "God is unfair asking of us that which He is not willing to do Himself. He asks us to sacrifice when He Himself is unwilling to sacrifice. Who made Him God anyway? It is time for a change in the government of the universe."

God could have destroyed Lucifer immediately; but had He done so, doubts would have remained forever in the minds of heavenly beings. In all fairness God must give him a chance to show just where his principles would lead. Accordingly Satan and approximately one third of the angels of heaven who followed him were cast out. "He was cast out into the earth, and his angels were cast out with him." Revelation 12:9.

Jesus described Satan's fall. "And he said unto them, I beheld Satan as lightning fall from heaven." Luke 10:18. Unfortunately for us, he has made this earth his home. This world has been getting a demonstration for the past six thousand years of just what the principles of God's enemy, Satan, will do when given a chance to grow. Satan immediately began to sow weeds among the good seed which God had placed upon this earth. He tempted Eve to sin, speaking to her through a serpent in the Garden of Eden. He lied to her by contradicting God and promising, "Ye shall not surely die."

Satan reserved his greatest temptations for his earthly confrontation with Jesus Christ Himself. Of Jesus the Bible says, "And he was there in the wilderness forty days, tempted of

Satan." Mark 1:13. All through Christ's life Satan assailed Him on every possible point, endeavoring to find a weak place in His spiritual armor. He "was in all points tempted like as we are, yet without sin." (Hebrews 4:15.)

In these last days of earth's history, just preceding the coming of our Lord, Satan's special attacks are reserved for a people who are endeavoring to serve God—Christian commandment-keepers. "Then the dragon was angry with the woman, and went off to make war on the rest of her offspring, on those who keep the commandments of God and bear testimony to Jesus." Revelation 12:17, R.S.V. You may expect that if you are endeavoring to keep all the commandments of God and if you bear testimony to the goodness of Jesus Christ, believing on Him with all your heart and accepting Him as your own Lord and Saviour, you will be a special object of Satan's last-day attacks.

The only way to meet the challenge of Satan is the method Christ used. To each of the three temptations with which Satan assailed Him in the wilderness, Christ replied, "It is written." God's Written Word was a part of His life. The Word of God must be our bulwark and defense. It is our only shield against the darts of the enemy. In following it we shall find our only safety. We must, above all else, always be willing to obey the commandments of God.

Thus we learn where suffering comes from. God is not responsible for it any more than the householder who sowed good seed but was greeted by weeds when the seed sprouted.

Soon Satan's demonstration will be complete. God will intervene and put an end to it all, and Satan will then be eternally destroyed. To him God says, "I will bring thee to ashes upon the earth in the sight of all them that behold thee. . . . Never shalt thou be any more." Ezekiel 28:18, 19. When God sends down fire out of heaven upon the wicked, Satan and all his followers will be reduced to ashes upon this earth. This will be his final destruction in the fires of hell. And we have been promised that "affliction shall not rise up the second time." (Nahum 1:9.)

The day will come, thank God, when the weeds will be gone forever, and only the good grain will grow in God's universe. At that time "God shall wipe away all tears from their eyes; and there shall be no more death, neither sorrow, nor crying, neither shall there be any more pain: for the former things are passed away. And he that sat upon the throne said, Behold, I make all things new." Revelation 21:4, 5.

Do you want to have a place with God after sin is forever put away? Then place your life in the hands of the Lord Jesus Christ now. He will save you.

You need not be overcome by Satan, despite his clever wiles and devices. A simple old-time preacher used to describe in this way the situation in which we find ourselves: "Life is like an election in which three votes are cast. God votes for you, and the devil votes against you. Whichever way you vote decides the election!" How will you vote in the great controversy between Christ and Satan, on the side of God or Satan?

As for me, I take my stand with my heavenly Father and with His Son, my Saviour, who died in my place on Calvary. Will you join me?

5

STEPS TO PERSONAL PEACE

I WAS VISITING Death Row in Ohio State Penitentiary, with two sets of bars separating me from the condemned man whom I had come to meet for the first time. He was scheduled to die in the electric chair a few days later for a brutal killing in connection with an armed robbery.

My visit followed months of correspondence which had been mainly concentrated on Bible study. Though Sam Tannyhill's happy and at-peace-with-the-world attitude was exactly what his letters had led me to expect, yet as I witnessed it in person, I was truly astonished. Perhaps I betrayed by the look on my face or through some incautious word the way I truly felt concerning his approaching date with violent death. Reassuring me quickly, he said, "Pastor, I'm the happiest man in the world." To my inquiry as to how he could say that in view of the event which faced him, he replied, "When I was out there in the street, I had no hope; but since coming here I have found Jesus Christ as my Lord and Saviour. Now what happens to me in the next few days doesn't matter very much. It's what happens to me 'over there' that really counts. And I have all the hope in the world for 'over there.'"

Here was an amazing young man. Because of legal appeals, six dates had been set for his execution and five of them passed by, thus prolonging his life an extra year. I was with him when he died at the age of twenty-seven, paying the full price demanded by the state for his crime. I was not very brave that night as we stepped from the cell in the Death House, where we had spent the last three hours of his life. Together we entered the execution room with the twelve ashen witnesses and four nervous guards, all with eyes focused on the stark, polished-wood electric chair. I might gladly have exchanged my place with any other clergyman in the world just then, but I was there because Sam considered me his pastor and wanted me there. It was a responsibility I could not shirk. Sam died meekly, without a word, perfectly resigned to whatever should happen to his life.

Just before the appointed hour we had prayed together, this boy and I. He who had never seen the inside of a church in all his life and who had never held a Bible in his hands until a year before, had come to know God, and he offered extemporaneously a beautiful prayer that I shall always remember. "Lord," he prayed, "You know that one year ago I placed my life in Your hands. You know that nothing that has happened in this past year has changed that fact. Nothing that will happen tonight will change it either. My life is still in Your hands. Do with it as You see best. And, God, I know that You never make any mistakes. Amen."

After I had petitioned our heavenly Father, Sam prayed again, for he had forgotten something. "God," he pleaded, "do not hold these men responsible for what they are about to do. Remember, God, it's what I did that makes it necessary for them to take my life. If their act is a sin, Lord, charge it up to my account and then forgive it as You have forgiven all of my sins."

I silently wished that others might have shared the inspiration of hearing the two humble, heartfelt, and dedicated prayers which God and I heard that night. Truly Sam Tannyhill had been converted. Everyone who had any contact with him for the last year of his life in that prison knew it, and everyone respected him for it.

What had brought about this complete change? How did a young man who had traveled the road of crime to its logical and inevitable terminus—murder—who had spent most of his adult years in prison, ever make such a complete and thorough right-about-face? The change took place shortly after Sam had arrived on Death Row. A Bible had been given him, and he enrolled in the free Bible correspondence course offered by the television program Faith for Today.

In his Bible he began to read, for the first time, about a most marvelous Person named Jesus Christ. Gradually he came to see that this Christ offered exactly what he so much needed—forgiveness and cleansing from awful guilt and remorse. Under deep conviction and with the enormity of his sins resting heavily upon his conscience, he paced back and forth in his cell one Tuesday. At the end of the day Sam decided to pray—something he had never before done in his life. But he laughingly told me later that he felt his first prayer never went higher than the prison's roof, for he prayed for a gun with which to shoot his way out of Death Row, so that he could "go straight" on the outside. But no gun descended from the heavens!

For the next four days Sam continued to pace his cell, sometimes with tears coursing down his face. Just at sundown on Saturday night he prayed again, a different kind of prayer this time. Kneeling by the side of his narrow prison cot, he named every sin he could remember, asking God to forgive each one. Then he concluded with the plea, "Dear Lord, forgive me for every other sin that exists, because I know I'm guilty of all of them." After that, for the first time that he could remember, he found peace. And he slept "like a baby."

Sam's life was completely changed. He studied his Bible with unparalleled enthusiasm, spending an average of five hours a day with this Book which he came to love. I felt that he became a giant in his understanding of the Scriptures. He committed to memory many whole Bible chapters. As the Word of God became a living part of his experience, his outlook mellowed and his life became purposeful. In the months that followed no one ever had occasion to doubt that what God had done for Sam Tannyhill was real and permanent.

I have seen many lives changed similarly. I know from personal observation and experience that God can change men today just as completely as He changed Saul of Tarsus into Paul, the great and mighty apostle to the Gentiles. Furthermore, this change always follows the same basic steps, even though the circumstances of each life differ. You too can take these steps; you too can be a different person if you really want to be. You can be as different as day is from night, for "if any man be in Christ, he is a new creature: old things are passed away; behold, all things are become new." (2 Corinthians 5:17.)

What are these steps Sam took, which any other willing person may take? First of all, obviously, Sam came to feel his need and was completely dissatisfied with his life. Recognizing the awful sinfulness of his past, he came to vehemently hate it; and he deeply longed for something better.

Have you ever felt like that? Could it be possible that you feel that way even now? Then there is hope for you. You have already taken the first step. Nothing much can be done for a man who is completely satisfied with himself and his way of life. No genuine and lasting change can possibly take place until he sees himself as he really is and longs to be better. Were he to stop here, however, he would become an emotional wreck, for he would live the rest of his life under the impossible weight of overwhelming guilt and remorse. No person can do that indefinitely without serious damaging effects to his entire person—mental and physical.

Our dissatisfaction with our past must lead us to a desire to see something done about it. Unfortunately, however, nothing that we can do will change the past. This is where we need the help of Someone greater than ourselves, and here is where God has promised to aid us. The step in Sam's life which followed his sorrow for his sins was confession—confession of all known sins to God. And this step every soul must take. "If we confess our sins, he is faithful and just to forgive us our sins, and to cleanse us from all unrighteousness." 1 John 1:9.

This is a wonderful promise, encouraging us to confess our guilt to the One who can forgive us and cleanse us from all our past mistakes and sins. Notice that whether or not a person *feels* forgiven is entirely immaterial. Some, like Sam, do; others do not. How we *feel* about the matter has nothing to do with whether or not God keeps His promise. We must believe that we are forgiven because we can trust Him to keep His word.

The third step we must take is one which Sam took joyfully and wholeheartedly. It is the step of belief. The Apostle Paul took that step more than 1,900 years ago, and here is what he from his experience tells us about it: "If thou shalt confess with thy mouth the Lord Jesus, and shalt believe in thine heart that God hath raised him from the dead, thou shalt be saved. For with the heart man believeth unto righteousness; and with the mouth confession is made unto salvation." Romans 10:9, 10. Our salvation will be effected because of what Jesus Christ did for us on Calvary. There He paid the awful price for our sins—He died in our place. His blood covers our sins and cleanses us. We must believe that He died for us and that because God raised Him from the dead, He lives today in heaven. We must believe that someday He will come again to take us home to Himself.

The next step is not for us to take; God takes it for us. Jesus spoke of it one night to Nicodemus, a ruler of the Pharisees. To him He said, "Ye must be born again." John 3:7. Nicodemus questioned how such a thing could be possible, but the Saviour made clear that He was speaking of a spiritual experience: "That which is born of the flesh is flesh; and that which is born of the Spirit is spirit." Verse 6.

We call this experience "the new birth." It is something God does for us. Here is how He explains it to us: "A new heart also will I give you, and a new spirit will I put within you: and I will take away the stony heart out of your flesh, and I will give you an heart of flesh. And I will put my spirit within you, and cause you to walk in my statutes, and ye shall keep my judgments, and do them." Ezekiel 36:26, 27.

If you will take these steps, allowing God to give you the experience of the new birth, your life will show, as Sam's did, a change. And you, like him, will have hope for the future. The immediate present will not matter. You, too, will be able to say, "It's what happens to me 'over there' that counts. And I have all the hope in the world for 'over there.'"

When the execution was over that night and the witnesses and guards had left the room, I was alone with Sam. He was still seated in the electric chair. The belts and electrodes and the black face mask had all been removed. As I looked down into his dead face, I thought of what he had said to me just twenty minutes earlier. Taking me by the hand and putting another hand on my shoulder, he had said, "Pastor, I'll be looking for you over there." And I had replied from a heart full of real conviction, "I know that you'll be there, Sam; and by God's grace, so will I." Clasping my hand a little tighter and gripping my shoulder firmly, he said, "Good-bye then; I'll see you in the morning."

That night we made an appointment to meet—as real as any appointment I have ever made in my life—an appointment to meet "in the morning." The morning of the coming of our Lord, the resurrection morning, the morning of reunion. By God's grace I intend to keep that appointment.

It is a wonderful thing to have hope in Christ in this life. I cannot imagine what those do who do not have it. That night with Sam I was grateful for my faith and for what it had done for him and for me. I am still grateful for it. I could not live without it. Do you have hope and faith in Christ? If not, would you like to have it? Would you like to have constant peace in the knowledge of full and free forgiveness? Does a hope for the future appeal to you? Then take the steps! Take them now! Give your heart and life to the Lord Jesus Christ. In complete dedication of life and heart let Him make you into a new person. You will never regret it.

6

WHAT HEAVEN IS LIKE

"THERE IS no such thing as heaven. When you are dead, you're dead, and that's all!" Spoken as they were to those who mourned a very recent loss, these words were cruel and heartless. Though fifteen years have passed, I have never forgotten those words, for they were spoken to my own family as some of us talked of the hope which Christians have in God and heaven. Afterward, when those of us who believed were alone again, we affirmed anew how glad we were for our faith in the hereafter.

What has caused many people to reject the entire idea of heaven? Why do some persist in scoffingly referring to it as "pie in the sky by and by"? My relative's declaration of unbelief made me ask myself this question again and again. Could it be that perhaps we who believe have been somewhat out of touch with modern life and the needs of twentieth-century humanity in our emphasis on certain aspects of heaven? Let me show you what I mean.

A number of years ago I heard an excellent preacher discuss the hereafter before a sizable audience. He read verses from the Bible which speak of heaven's Holy City as being a very real and very beautiful place, of its having glorious streets of gold

46

and walls of jasper and told how appealing that sounded to him. I recall that he spent considerable time in describing the grapes which he felt will be grown there, asserting that they will be huge and the most delicious we have ever eaten. He read other Bible verses which seem to indicate that the climate of heaven will be just right, with no bitter winter cold or exhausting summer heat. He was eloquent in his description of the music of heaven and said that he intended to spend the first thousand years of eternity in studying music, concentrating especially on the harp, which he suggested was the instrument of heaven. It was all very real to him, and I was impressed by his sincerity.

When it was all over, I tried to analyze my own reactions. I had no desire to dispute any of his points, but I had to admit that he had not really awakened in my heart a favorable response. I decided on the reason, and reverently but realistically I want to share my conclusions with you.

Streets of gold would be nice to have, I presume, but I have never really missed them or even longed for them, for in my neighborhood we are getting along nicely with streets made of plain black asphalt. And I have never felt a need for walls of jasper around my town. In fact, I am just as glad not to have any walls at all. In the little suburban Long Island community where I live, not even a sign shows when one leaves one town and enters the next. A wall, no matter how lovely, would not be a basic need of a modern man who does not even feel the need of a definitive sign on the town line.

And speaking about luscious grapes and a salubrious climate, I remember a long-distance telephone call which a number of years ago brought me a tempting invitation to pastor a fine and influential church. My inquiry regarding opportunities to pursue some of my particular special interests in church work met with no response. As a compensation, however, I was told that accepting this invitation would result in our living in the area of the finest climate in the United States, with the very finest fresh fruits and vegetables constantly at our disposal.

No opportunities to work in the area of service I loved best—but a fine climate! I tried not to show it, but inwardly I felt insulted! Work *unhappily* in the best climate available? Not me! I would sooner take the worst weather in the world if need be (not that Long Island has it) and all the handicaps of eating out of cans (I'm not doing that, either) if my work can offer me a challenge and my daily life can be happy.

Life is more than climate. Jesus Himself recognized this same principle when He said, "A man's life consisteth not in the abundance of the things which he possesseth." And of course it doesn't! Streets of gold, walls of jasper, delectable grapes, an excellent climate, are all fine—but not enough in themselves to make me want to leave the relative happiness which I have here and now. And at the risk of being different, I will admit that as yet I have developed no real burden to learn to play a harp. Someday I might have a different feeling about that; but now it does not meet any persistent longing of my life. I listened to eight harps playing an entire concert once, and the memory of those two long hours will last me for a long time.

Perhaps others have reacted similarly when only these aspects of heaven have been presented, and have even rejected the whole idea of that kind of heaven. The truth of the matter, as I see it, is that these things are just the additional fringe benefits, if you please, of the *life* which the Bible describes for us in the hereafter God is preparing for the saved of the earth. Now let us examine what the Bible teaches about that life.

Very few individuals have ever claimed to have actually seen heaven, but the prophet John tells us that God gave him this privilege. "And I saw a new heaven and a new earth." Revelation 21:1. What does this man who looked into heaven itself have to say about it? What is his first response regarding it? "There was no more sea." A strange first reaction indeed—until you think about it. And then it becomes exceedingly meaningful. John had been banished to the desolate and barren Isle of Patmos, where he lived his lonely years in exile and solitude. Undoubtedly on many occasions he watched the restless waves lap monotonously against the shoreline of the island and looked out longingly as far as his aging eyes could see toward his homeland. That was where his loved ones were—on the other side of the sea.

The sea separated him from everything and everyone that could make life happy for him. The first thing he noticed about heaven, therefore, was the absence of the sea. He observed joyfully not the gold and the jasper, but the fact that in heaven there is nothing to separate a man from his loved ones and from his work and from the opportunities that bring genuine daily happiness to him. In heaven nothing prevents a man from achieving absolute fulfillment, and that begins to mean something to me, too. This simple observation of John gives me something with which I can identify. Death is a great sea that separates loved ones. So do misunderstanding, wasted opportunities, mistakes in judgment. I can respond affirmatively to the idea that in heaven there will be "no more sea."

John continued, "And God shall wipe away all tears from their eyes; and there shall be no more death, neither sorrow, nor crying, neither shall there be any more pain: for the former things are passed away." Revelation 21:4. That hits "pay dirt" with me! These are the things which rob all life, including mine, of joy and beauty. These are the constant and persistent enemies of all that is worthwhile for all of us. I respond wholeheartedly and completely to the idea that they will be done away with forever in the future life God desires me to have.

Most of what the Bible says about heaven is written in the negative, telling us strongly and encouragingly about what will *not* be there—no more death, sorrow, crying, pain. I used to be disturbed somewhat by this because good pedagogy would dictate that such a description should be presented in the affirmative. Why this emphasis, then, upon the negative?

Perhaps God faced certain unresolvable problems and serious limitations in describing heaven to us in any other terms. How would you describe a warm island in the tropical Caribbean to an Eskimo who had had few opportunities to travel? You might begin by telling him that islands in the sun have palm trees. But what would this mean to a man whose world consists mostly of frozen waters?

Before long, in spite of yourself, you would be drawing on the negative, perhaps saying something like this: "Caribbean islands have no polar bears, no freezing temperatures, no ice, no snow, no need for trapping wild beasts to secure warm fur garments." Do you see the direction you would be forced to take because of the Eskimo's lack of understanding regarding the tropics? Even greater is the problem faced by God in describing heaven to us. He has told us, "Eye hath not seen, nor ear heard, neither have entered into the heart of man, the things which God hath prepared for them that love him." 1 Corinthians 2:9. We have nothing to compare to it.

Much of the present-day emphasis on heaven has stressed the idea of *rest*. To some this may sound most inviting—perhaps to the aged or the chronically ill or those especially weary because of unusual manual labor. But frankly, this does not sound especially attractive to me. I might like a few days of relaxation and rest when I first get to heaven, but I am the kind of individual who can hardly stand two weeks of vacation spent in one place with nothing to do but "rest." In a very short time that is not enjoyable for me anymore. What would I ever do with the ceaseless ages of all eternity on my hands? I am glad that God has planned something different.

Instead of sitting about in everlasting relaxed inactivity, those who ultimately reach heaven will enjoy a fruitful life. "And they shall build houses, and inhabit them; and they shall plant vineyards, and eat the fruit of them. They shall not build, and another inhabit; they shall not plant, and another eat: for as the days of a tree are the days of my people, and mine elect shall long enjoy the work of their hands. They shall not labour in vain, nor bring forth for trouble; for they are the seed of the blessed of the Lord, and their offspring with them." Isaiah 65:

21-23. I can engage in an endless variety of satisfying labor which will not be done in vain. And no trouble! I can stand an eternity of freedom from trouble.

All God's creation will be restored to the peace and harmony that He intended for it in the beginning. Even the animal kingdom will show the tranquillity, the lack of hostility and aggressiveness, which God originally intended for His whole creation. "The wolf and the lamb shall feed together, and the lion shall eat straw like the bullock. . . . They shall not hurt nor destroy in all my holy mountain, saith the Lord." Verse 25. I respond to a world with a life like that.

I make no apologies for my belief in heaven. The place described in God's Word promises me just the kind of life I have always wanted to live. And God assures me I will be happy—happy forever, every day and every hour of my life. "For, behold, I create new heavens and a new earth: and the former shall not be remembered, nor come into mind. But be ye glad and rejoice for ever in that which I create: for, behold, I create Jerusalem a rejoicing, and her people a joy." Verses 17, 18. Heaven completely fits my basic needs. It sounds like *my* country. Its people sound like *my* people. Because of this I can feel with certainty that "heaven is my home."

If everyone knew what heaven is really like, would not each desire a place there, too? It would seem so. There is room enough for *all*. God has made provision for every individual who desires a place in His eternal kingdom. "For God so loved the world, that he gave his only begotten Son, that whosoever believeth in him should not perish, but have everlasting life." John 3:16. Christ's death on the cross has paid the price for every one of us. We may have everlasting life through Him if we accept the blood shed for us on Calvary.

Then as we go through life, we will want to be obedient to the principles which our heavenly Father and His Son, Jesus Christ, have outlined for us in God's Word, the Bible. This obedience will call for a deliberate shunning of some of the so-called pleasures of the world. In this sense it will cost us something. But without doubt, when we finally get on the other side, we will all agree that heaven is cheap enough.

And so I look forward confidently to the future. Many things about the hereafter I do not know and cannot understand, and they may never be made plain to me until I finally get there. But I have no fear about these things. Although I do not know all, I have the assurance that God does. He has made the plans for me, and I can safely trust in Him.

"I said to the man who stood at the gate, . . . 'Give me a light that I may tread safely into the unknown.' And he replied, 'Go out into the darkness and put your hand into the hand of God. That shall be to you better than light and safer than a known way.'" With my hand in the hand of God, I walk happily through life, looking forward to heaven, my home. Will you join me?

SOME EVENTS GOD FORETOLD

MY WIFE and I and some friends attended a concert one evening. It had been a long time since we had been able to do anything like this, and we enjoyed it tremendously. A number of excellent musical organizations took part, but the program was lengthy. After a time we grew weary and restless and fell to wondering if the concert would ever end. We concluded, and correctly, that it had about ten more minutes to go.

Had we shared our conclusion with those around us, someone might have questioned the accuracy of our prediction. He might even have expostulated, "The program has gone on now for three hours. They're singing just as energetically and enthusiastically now as they did at the beginning. What makes you feel that it will end in ten minutes?" To which we might have replied, "We have been following the printed program which all of us were given when we entered. The numbers presented have not deviated in any way from what was outlined in advance. The concluding number is now being presented, and without doubt within ten minutes the program will end."

Do you realize that God has given to all of us *in advance* a program of world events so that we may know just where we are living in time? And are you aware that the events which have taken place down through the years have corresponded exactly to this prophetic program which God made available to the human family in the Bible long ago? And do you know that according to this program we are living in the very closing days of earth's history—in the last ten minutes of "the concert"? Do you realize the significance of the fact that the very next event on the program is the second coming of Jesus Christ to this earth to bring salvation to those who are looking for Him?

When Jesus was here upon this earth, He talked often of His second coming. One day He was asked, "Tell us, when shall these things be? and what shall be the sign of thy coming, and of the end of the world?" Matthew 24:3. Jesus had just finished telling His disciples about the desolation and destruction which would come to Jerusalem. They jumped to the conclusion that this could happen only when the world itself ended. The Master did not tell them all He might have—that Jerusalem would be destroyed soon, but that many hundreds of years would pass before His second advent. Their comprehension was too limited to grasp this. So He talked of both events together, answering both their questions, even though they thought they had asked only one.

He said, "Ye shall hear of wars and rumours of wars: see that ye be not troubled: for all these things must come to pass, but the end is not yet. For nation shall rise against nation, and kingdom against kingdom: and there shall be famines, and pestilences, and earthquakes, in divers places. All these are the beginning of sorrows." Matthew 24:6-8. He drew back the veil to allow them to peer dimly into the future, but mercifully He showed them very little.

Could they ever have been able to stand the shock, had He described to them wars which would involve atom blasts destroying great cities and thousands of people in an instant? With their limited vision, could they ever have comprehended, not just one nation rising against another, but rather most of the world lined up in two armed camps, each side possessing the power to destroy all of mankind? And could they have visualized these armed camps being deterred from its use only by the realization that destruction of the enemy might mean self-destruction as well?

But they needed certain specifics, certain definite and positive answers to their questions, and He gave them these. He said, "And there shall be signs in the sun, and in the moon, and in the stars; . . . for the powers of heaven shall be shaken. And then shall they see the Son of man coming in a cloud with power and great glory." Luke 21:25-27.

And Christ was even more specific about just when these heavenly signs would take place. He explained, "Immediately after the tribulation of those days shall the sun be darkened, and the moon shall not give her light, and the stars shall fall from heaven." Matthew 24:29. God's church and people went through a time of persecution and tribulation which lasted for hundreds of years and corresponded accurately with a prophecy given in the Book of Revelation regarding these events. The terminology used by Christ and quoted by Matthew is fascinating, for Matthew indicated that *immediately* after this persecution ceased, these signs of the heavens would take place. History tells us that this persecution almost wholly ended about the middle of the eighteenth century. And then, right on time, the signs of His coming in the heavens at once began to appear.

Practically everyone knows about the extraordinary darkness which began at midday on May 19, 1780. Even Webster's *Dictionary* describes it under the title "dark day." The poet Whittier speaks of it in his poem "Abraham Davenport":

> " 'Twas on a May-day of the far old year
> Seventeen hundred eighty, that there fell
> Over the bloom and sweet life of the Spring,
> Over the fresh earth and the heaven of noon,
> A horror of great darkness. . . .
> Birds ceased to sing, and all the barnyard fowls

> Roosted; the cattle at the pasture bars
> Lowed, and looked homeward; bats on leathern wings
> Flitted abroad; the sounds of labor died;
> Men prayed, and women wept; all ears grew sharp
> To hear the doom-blast of the trumpet shatter
> The black sky."

It fascinates me to realize that men who were students of Bible prophecy were specifically looking for these signs in the heavens and felt that the time had come for them to be seen. In 1762 Edmund March, a man bearing a master of arts degree from Harvard University, wrote, "If we could find the Signs in the Sun, and in the Moon, and in the Stars; particularly the Sun darkened, the Moon withholding her Light, and the Stars of Heaven fallen, we should be ready perhaps to think of the Coming of the Son of Man just at hand: For upon the Earth is Distress of Nations, with perplexity, the Sea and the Waves roaring."

Many others were watching for these signs, and when the unexplained darkness of May 19, 1780, occurred, and when that same night the moon, instead of giving her ordinary color, was blood red, many indeed were the individuals who recognized this as a sign of the coming of the Lord.

Benjamin Gorton, a merchant and president of the Village Trustees of Troy, New York, said in a published work of 1808: "Now let us examine if this is not the generation" in which those literal signs were to take place. Then he continued, "The sun was remarkably darkened in 1780, 28 years last May. In Providence, Rhode-Island, it commenced in the forenoon, so that the cows returned from pasture as at evening, and fowls went to roost; candles lighted in order to see to do business; and many people much disturbed in their minds for the event.

"At Conway, Massachusetts, they dined by candle-light; and farmers were obliged to leave their sowing, and other work, in the field, for want of light. At Fishkill, New-York, in the afternoon business was, in part, laid by, by reason of darkness; all appeared to be tinged with a yellow hue. This appears to be the first particular sign spoken of apparent to the natural eye immediately: the second is that of the moon's turning to blood; this I have not seen, but, from information, I have reason to believe it did take place between 2 o'clock and day break in the morning of the same night after which the sun was darkened, which was said to appear as a clotter of blood; and it is the more probable, as that night, before the moon appeared, was as dark, in proportion, as the day, and of course would give the moon an extraordinary appearance—not suffering her to give her light." He immediately added, "The next in course, it seems, is the falling of the stars from heaven."

And the expected event came just when it should have, in its exact order in Bible prophecy. On the night of November 12-13, 1833, occurred a meteoric shower which was the most remarkable of its kind on record. A modern Harvard astronomer, W. J. Fisher, describes it in these words: "In the early morning of November 13, 1833, the people of the United States were waked by early risers to turn out and see the stars fall. And fall they did—silently, singly, in bursts and sheaves, tiny ones and balls like the moon. All the observers saw that the meteors darted away from a single point in the sky [in the constellation Leo]; the meteors 'were like the ribs of a gigantic umbrella.' So plain was this that two quite amateur observers made sketches, . . . so far as we know the only drawings of the phenomenon that have survived."

The French astronomer Flammarion says that the density of the star shower compared to "half the number of flakes which we perceive in the air during an ordinary shower of snow." Another observer described the meteors as being thick as snowflakes. Peter M. Millman wrote in *The Telescope*, May-June, 1940, that estimates for the number of shooting stars visible at one place vary from ten thousand to two hundred thousand an hour.

The American Indians were so impressed by the spectacle of the falling stars that they recorded the event on their simple calendars. In southern Arizona several small tribes of Indians known collectively as the Pimas lived long before the coming of the white man. They have long had the reputation of being among the most civilized of all North American Indians. Their tribal name has been conferred on the variety of cotton known as Pima, developed in their area and widely grown elsewhere. The Pima Indians invented a "calendar stick," a length of wood on which they carved pictures illustrating what they considered to be the outstanding event of each year. The very first picture on the oldest Pima calendar stick is a group of eight meteorites to represent the year 1833. The falling of the stars made such an impression upon the Pima Indians that it became the first recorded event in their tribal history.

Everyone who knew anything about the prophecies of the Scriptures was made to think seriously about the significance of these heavenly signs, and this is just as God had planned it. Henry J. Pickering, editor of *The Old Countryman*, a New York City weekly, described the falling of the stars, which had happened just the day before, and then said, "Many things now occurring upon the earth tend to convince us that we are in the 'latter days.' This exhibition we deem to be a type of an awful day fast hurrying upon us. This is our sincere opinion; and what we think, we are not ashamed to tell."

Looked at against the backdrop of the six thousand years of earth's history, we may well say that we are living in the last "ten minutes" of God's program for man on earth. And what is the next great event on the program? "And then shall they see the Son of man coming in a cloud with power and great glory." Luke 21:27. I am glad I have the printed program. And I am glad I have read it, studied it, and believed it. My faith is strengthened by the fact that it has not failed in a single particular—everything has happened exactly according to plan. And now that I have seen some of the last events, I have no doubt whatsoever but that the final event on the program is about to take place. Soon Jesus will come again.

Have you ever visited a ghost town, a town which once was lived in, but is now deserted? It is a strange thing to walk down the empty streets, trying to imagine the pulsating life which once made the town look and seem alive. I went through such a town a short time ago in the western part of the United States. It had been lived in right up until a few years ago. Its existence had been primarily dependent on the profits received from working a large mine nearby. But changing times had made the operation of the mine unprofitable, and as the result, everyone in the town had moved away. The only ones left behind were in the cemetery, but they were unable to communicate.

Certain features about the stores indicated that at one time they had meant a great deal to those who owned them. Billboards and other advertising signs attempted to attract customers to businesses which no longer existed. At one time these stores and residences represented everything of value in the lives of those who owned them. But the day came when these things meant little or nothing, and the owners left them and went elsewhere.

As I walked about the streets of the ghost town, seeing how little the ordinary pursuits of life had come to mean to those who had dwelt there, I mused that someday all the ordinary values of life will mean just that little, for business, gold, houses, lands, prestige, profits, and money in the bank are all temporary, transitory, in their rewards. Someday all of them are going to be wiped out.

It must have been the realization of this that made Peter exclaim, "Seeing then that all these things shall be dissolved, what manner of persons ought ye to be in all holy conversation and godliness, looking for and hasting unto the coming of the day of God, wherein the heavens being on fire shall be dissolved, and the elements shall melt with fervent heat? Nevertheless we, according to his promise, look for new heavens and a new earth, wherein dwelleth righteousness." 2 Peter 3:11-13.

I therefore believe that Jesus is coming again. I believe it more now than I ever did. According to His promise I, too, "look for new heavens and a new earth, wherein dwelleth righteousness."

The only ones who can look forward to the coming of Christ with joy are those who expect to benefit by it. I have heard people say, "I believe that Jesus is coming again, but I hope it will not be in my day." Such persons are not prepared to meet Jesus. They have not made love for Him supreme in their experience. They have not made the second advent of our Lord the goal and culminating point of life, and therefore they have only fear as they see the day approaching.

The day of Christ's coming should be as the day of harvest to one who has planted and cultivated. It should be as the day of deliverance to a prisoner. It should be looked forward to as a day of coronation of the King, the day of marriage to the bride. When once you realize that the coming of the Lord will be as a Ransomer to redeem you from sin and its effects, to subdue all the enemies that have brought frustrations of life to you, and as a Friend to comfort you, then you, with the prophet John, will be able to say with joy and gladness, "Come, Lord Jesus."

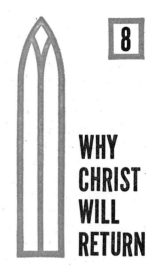

8

WHY CHRIST WILL RETURN

ARRIVING HOME one evening, my wife and I happily discovered a letter from our daughter in college. I suppose no matter how often she wrote, we would wish to hear from her more frequently. While we try to be understanding when a letter arrives, it is hard for either of us to accept anything but the very latest rapid reading techniques in the other.

Her letter on this occasion told of the daily round of college activities and then inquired about her "little brother" (incidentally, by then considerably taller than she), offering the comment, "I surely do miss that fellow." And that little statement started us on a bit of reminiscing about the time when her brother was just a few days old and she was not quite three.

Early in the morning our little girl had called smugly from her bed for "Mommy." But because at the moment Mommy was busy with the new baby, I had to substitute temporarily—something which fathers find at times to be extremely difficult. In the past our little girl had found that a request for "Mommy" had without exception brought her mother quickly to her. But this time was different, and her father badly bungled the job of telling her that mother was busy just now taking care of little

61

brother. My further explanation that Mommy now had to give time to both her children could not be comprehended, and to my consternation, it produced unexpected tears. When in clumsy desperation I argued, "Aren't you glad that you have a baby brother?" this capped the climax. In complete desolation she wailed, "I don't *need* a baby brother!"

She didn't know it then, but our little girl did need a baby brother, to keep her from being spoiled by doting parents, to teach her to share, and to provide the companionship and admiration she has received from her brother all through her growing-up years. Similarly, many of life's genuine needs are little appreciated or comprehended even by us who are older.

One of the Bible's greatest writers understood our lack of comprehension in this area. Paul wrote in Romans 8:26, "We know not what we should pray for as we ought." Therefore God, as a loving Parent, has prepared certain things for us which we may not even realize we need.

Take for instance the second advent of our Lord Jesus Christ in the clouds of heaven. How many ordinary run-of-the-mill people you might meet on the street sense a need for Jesus to return to this earth again? Most reason that they are getting along very well and fear that the coming of the Lord might "spoil it all." I wonder if our loving God does not smile indulgently at our lack of understanding, even as we do when small children boldly make declarations quite out of touch with reality.

Why is the Lord coming back again? Admittedly perfect understanding is reserved until on the other side God opens our eyes completely to His eternal purposes. But God has revealed some things to us now which we can grasp. Paul refers to the coming of Christ as our "blessed hope," and if more people understood the facts about His coming as revealed in Scripture, it would be more widely considered as such.

X One paramount reason for the coming of Jesus concerns those righteous ones we have "loved long since and lost awhile" who will be raised to life again. Here are the exact words of the promise, as gripping and dramatic as any ever made since the world began: "Marvel not at this: for the hour is coming, in the which all that are in the graves shall hear his voice, and shall come forth." John 5:28, 29. No one who has ever lost a dear one through death could ever feel that he did not *need* the resurrection. Once he really comprehends that Christ's coming will raise the dead and reunite families, the second advent becomes a "blessed hope" indeed.

What a marvelous thing it will be to meet personally and face to face the Christ who said of Himself, "I am the resurrection, and the life: he that believeth in me, though he were dead, yet shall he live: and whosoever liveth and believeth in me shall never die." John 11:25, 26. I have read those words often to sorrowing groups of people at an open grave. I have never failed to feel the thrill of that promise. My own heart responds with the hope that Christ will come *soon* to raise the dead.

The Christ who Himself has passed through the grave declares, "I am he that liveth, and was dead; and, behold, I am alive for evermore, Amen; and have the keys of hell and of death." Revelation 1:18. Absolute death, of course, would know no awaking; but Jesus broke death's power, and as the result we can refer confidently now to it as a sleep. Because Christ at His coming will raise the dead and reunite loved ones, I need His second advent.

A second promise of accomplishment at the Lord's coming is described in 1 Corinthians 15:51-53: "Behold, I shew you a mystery; We shall not all sleep, but we shall all be changed, in a moment, in the twinkling of an eye, at the last trump: for the trumpet shall sound, and the dead shall be raised incorruptible, and we shall be changed. For this corruptible must put on incorruption, and this mortal must put on immortality." "For this perishable nature must put on the imperishable," is the rendering of the Revised Standard Version.

It is difficult for us to comprehend the magnitude of this promise. How perishable are these bodies of ours at present! A person begins to get old just at the time when he ought to be ready to accomplish the most with his accumulated experience. But when Christ comes, He will make us "imperishable." Then, no longer subject to death, we will never grow old. Inherent in this promise is also the eternal obliteration of pain, sickness, sorrow, handicaps, death, and tears. "And God shall wipe away all tears from their eyes; and there shall be no more death, neither sorrow, nor crying, neither shall there be any more pain: for the former things are passed away." Revelation 21:4. How we all need this!

A third accomplishment of the Lord's coming has to do with the removal of distressing conditions in our world. Long ago Christ prophesied, "As it was in the days of Noe so shall it be also in the days of the Son of man. They did eat, they drank, they married wives, they were given in marriage, until the day that Noe entered into the ark, and the flood came, and destroyed them all. . . . Even thus shall it be in the day when the Son of man is revealed." Luke 17:26-30.

What were conditions like then? "And God saw that the wickedness of man was great in the earth, and that every imagination of the thoughts of his heart was only evil continually." "The earth also was corrupt before God, and the earth was filled with violence. And God looked upon the earth, and, behold, it was corrupt; for all flesh had corrupted his way upon the earth." Genesis 6:5, 11, 12. The violence, wickedness, and corrupted ways so prevalent today make us realize that conditions are not much different now from what they were in the days before the Flood.

Here is what God indicated the last days would be like: "This know also, that in the last days perilous times shall come. For men shall be lovers of their own selves, covetous, boasters, proud, blasphemers, disobedient to parents, unthankful, unholy, without natural affection, trucebreakers, false accusers, incontinent, fierce, despisers of those that are good, traitors, heady, highminded, lovers of pleasures more than lovers of God; having a form of godliness, but denying the power thereof: from such turn away." "But evil men and seducers shall wax worse and worse, deceiving, and being deceived." 2 Timothy 3:1-5, 13. Matthew Henry's comment is appropriate: "Even to the end of time there will still be occasion for the same complaint; the world will grow no better, no, not when it is drawing toward its period. That it is, and . . . it will be worst of all just before Christ's coming."

When Jesus comes, evildoers are to suffer the same fate which befell the wicked of Noah's day—destruction and death. "For yourselves know perfectly that the day of the Lord so cometh as a thief in the night. For when they shall say, Peace and safety; then sudden destruction cometh upon them, as travail upon a woman with child; and they shall not escape. But ye, brethren, are not in darkness, that that day should overtake you as a thief." 1 Thessalonians 5:2-4.

Every person who has ever suffered the results of sin in a broken home or in a broken body, every one who has ever suffered the effects of physical violence or the chicanery of ruthless, unscrupulous individuals, will certainly agree that the coming of the Lord is needed to change all this.

Moreover, His return will forever remove the redeemed from the temptations and allurements of Satan. Here is the promise in Revelation 20:1-3: "And I saw an angel come down from heaven, having the key of the bottomless pit and a great chain in his hand. And he laid hold on the dragon, that old serpent, which is the Devil, and Satan, and bound him a thousand years, and cast him into the bottomless pit, and shut him up, and set a seal upon him, that he should deceive the nations no more."

The righteous will then be safe beyond Satan's reach in God's Holy City, the New Jerusalem, and the time will come when Satan himself will be eternally destroyed. We are told that Jesus passed through the experience of death "that through death he might destroy him that had the power of death, that is, the devil." (Hebrews 2:14.) Here is Christ's promise: "In my Father's house are many mansions: if it were not so, I would have told

5

you. I go to prepare a place for you. And if I go and prepare a place for you, I will come again, and receive you unto myself; that where I am, there ye may be also." John 14:2, 3.

Although our understanding of the future may still be inadequate, the need of the coming of the Lord is apparent. How grateful I am that He has planned it in order to bring to me, along with all others who love His appearing, final and complete salvation with all of the saints forever. Personally, I look forward to Christ's coming with the greatest anticipation. I am happy to realize that it cannot be far off. I have in my heart an earnest desire to be completely dedicated to Him so that when He comes I can meet Him in peace, saying, "Lo, this is my God. I have waited for Him, and He will save me."

Is His coming also a blessed hope to you?

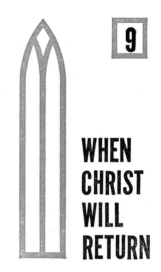

9

WHEN CHRIST WILL RETURN

ON A HOT, humid evening in Washington, D.C., I arrived late at a great religious service at Uline Arena. The crowd attending the meeting was so large that every seat seemed to be occupied in the huge auditorium. Finally one was found for me on the very last row, so far from the speaker's platform that recognition of those taking part was difficult.

Everyone seemed uncomfortable. The air was astir as those present sought relief from the high temperature by waving fans. The situation was so difficult that I and many others around me found it extremely hard to concentrate on the meeting's preliminaries. There was noise, with shuffling about as people tried to get comfortable. But all that seemed to change when an *a cappella* choir arose and began to sing. The selection was one I had never heard before but which I have heard many times since. A hush and a stillness such as I have rarely witnessed fell over that great congregation as the message of Christiansen's "Lost in the Night" began to reach the hearts of all. The message was simple enough, but perhaps because it said something that we all so thoroughly believed, it electrified me—"He is coming soon; Christ is coming soon!"

Particularly impressive to me that night was the part of the anthem in which a section of the choir sang over and over again, almost monotonously, the words, "He is coming soon," while the sopranos sang a lovely melody with altogether different words. But while the melody received its proper attention and was indeed properly prominent, it was almost eclipsed by the low urgency of the oft-repeated message given by the rest of the choir regarding the imminence of Christ's coming. That night the song became one of my favorites.

As I listened to the message of the song for the first time, I decided that in a sense it was representative of all life about us today. It is true that the ordinary melodies of life seem to go on day after day and year after year—not much different in most respects from those of previous centuries. But to one who knows and believes the teachings of the Bible the very air today seems charged with the low but urgent and oft-repeated undertone, "He is coming soon; He is coming soon."

Once you hear it, the undertone seems constant and insistent, and you hardly are able to hear anything else. Even the day-to-day melodies of life will become secondary as everything about you seems to cry out, "He is coming soon." You will wonder then, as I do now, how anyone could say in the disbelief described in the Scriptures, "Where is the promise of his coming? for since the fathers fell asleep, all things continue as they were from the beginning of the creation." 2 Peter 3:4. All things are not the same. Our day has the low, urgent, insistent undertone —growing in crescendo, at times almost drowning out all else— "He is coming soon."

Take, for instance, the "He is coming soon" being thundered out by the increase of knowledge and the rapid transportation of our day. Centuries ago the prophet Daniel had foretold that in the "time of the end" this world would see many running to and fro and knowledge greatly increased. (Daniel 12:4.) Centuries passed after Daniel wrote those words—centuries in which any change in man's way of life was almost imperceptible. A wheel turned only as fast for George Washington as it had for Alexander the Great, and Martha Washington was not able to make cloth for clothing any faster than those who made clothing for the Roman Caesars. But suddenly, with the utilization of steam and electricity, more changes were made in two generations than in all the thousands of years of previous human history put together.

After 1830 wheels began to turn faster. In fact, wheels and machines increased their tempo until now man can cover more distance in one day than he used to be able to in a lifetime! Recently I traveled from New York to Hong Kong, halfway around the world, in less time than it would have taken a man to go from New York to Philadelphia in 1787. And I was much less weary and travel worn. Now the age of electricity and steam is giving way to the atomic age with all the capacity for good and evil that it contains.

Talk about change—can we even begin to imagine how great have been the changes of the past few years? Can you imagine a world without automobiles, airplanes, diesel-powered railroad trains, ocean liners, fountain pens, automatic printing presses, matches, telegraphs, photography, sewing machines, anesthesia, telephones, typewriters, phonographs, linotypes, X rays, motion pictures, television, radios, and a host of other things? Can you imagine a world without electric lights or even electricity? Yet all these things upon which our daily mode of life depends were not known prior to 1800.

After centuries of sameness prior to that date, all of a sudden our world changed. Men began running to and fro with a speed and a frequency never known before. And just as the prophecy had predicted, knowledge was increased. But these things were to take place in "the time of the end." Do you hear the undertone? It is so loud that for me it drowns out almost everything else: "He is coming soon."

Jesus also taught that the last days would be characterized by "distress of nations, with perplexity." (Luke 21:25.) It is true that there have been times of distress and perplexity in the past. Our world has seen wars, at least one of which was so terrible that it lasted for thirty years. But would anyone want to challenge the idea that the distress and perplexity which *we* face is by far the greatest in man's history? Our world and its people today live under the very real threat of annihilation! No war could possibly last thirty years at present if all the destructive atomic forces which men have at their disposal should be unleashed. And even when no formally declared war exists, a new and strange thing called a "cold war" continues from day to day.

In Cuba, in the Congo, in Korea, in Russia, in China, in Vietnam, in Finland, in Angola, in South America, in Germany and all the rest of Europe, in Algiers, in Tibet, in India, in Japan, in the United States—people are living everywhere in a state of unrest, apprehension, and fear. At the United Nations one is made very much aware of this almost universal distress among nations, and one sees clearly the perplexity facing men everywhere. Never before has such a time been known. These are the "last days." What does all this say? Can you hear the undertone? It seems loud to me—"He is coming soon."

Can you see and hear the "He is coming soon" in this Biblical description of last-day events? "This know also, that in the last days perilous times shall come. For men shall be lovers of their own selves, covetous, boasters, proud, blasphemers, disobedient to parents, unthankful, unholy, without natural affection, trucebreakers, false accusers, incontinent, fierce, despisers of those that are good, traitors, heady, highminded, lovers of pleasures more than lovers of God; having a form of godliness, but denying the power thereof." 2 Timothy 3:1-5. What depths to which the human character will slip before Jesus comes!

Now compare this with what we see all about us. In the past few years since World War II, crime of all sorts has increased and continues to increase by leaps and bounds. The reports of J. Edgar Hoover, printed in the public press from time to time, are shocking and astounding. The statistics showing the year-by-year percentage advance of crime would be unbelievable if we did not have confidence in its source. Every day we hear of robberies, murders, swindles, election frauds, arson, and terrible violence of all sorts. Our courts and jails are filled with narcotic addicts, juvenile delinquents, racketeers.

The description of the earth in Noah's day seems applicable to our own: "The earth also was corrupt before God, and the earth was filled with violence." Genesis 6:11. Jesus Himself had prophesied, "As it was in the days of Noe, so shall it be also in the days of the Son of man." Luke 17:26. Divorces, drunkenness, frauds, and immorality have become commonplace to us. Because they are all about us in such abundance, they might seem in a sense to make up the fabric out of which life is woven. They do not seem flagrantly sinful anymore. And of what significance is all this? To one whose ear is tuned to God's Word the message comes through loud and clear: "He is coming soon."

Yet another tremendous and heartening fulfillment of prophecy indicates the nearness of the coming of the Lord. Jesus said, "And this gospel of the kingdom shall be preached in all the world for a witness unto all nations; and then shall the end come." Matthew 24:14. The inventions of our day have made the remotest corner of earth easily available by radio and television. Jet travel has made it seem as if the world has shrunk, and now missionaries have gone out to proclaim God's message everywhere. My own church is preaching the gospel in 189 countries, which represent 98.97 percent of the world's population. "He is coming soon."

But despite the fact that everything today points out that we are living in the last days and that Christ is coming soon, it is possible for us not to grasp fully the idea that He really is coming in our day. This is the truth that I want to emphasize: *We may well live to see Jesus come!* McCheyne, a Scottish preacher, once asked some friends, "Do you think Christ will come tonight?" One after another they replied, "I think not." When all had given the same answer, he solemnly repeated the text, "The

Son of man cometh at an hour when ye think not." The message bears repeating once again—"He is coming *soon*."

I am never able to visit the French-Canadian city of Quebec without thinking of an event which happened there many years ago. There on the Plains of Abraham the English troops of General Wolfe won Quebec from the French. When you see the steep ascent that Wolfe's men had to make up the face of the rocky cliffs, you are amazed that their bold venture ever succeeded. Any defenders should have been able to hold off armed men climbing such a cliff as that. Why then were they overcome? It was because they became careless and pleasure loving.

One night when the defenders were off guard, the forces of General Wolfe saw their opportunity, scaled the heights, and took the city. Quebec fell because its defenders failed to keep watch. We who guard the citadels of our souls would do well to remember the words of Christ, "Watch therefore: for ye know not what hour your Lord doth come. . . . Therefore be ye also ready: for in such an hour as ye think not the Son of man cometh." Matthew 24:42-44. Our only safety lies in getting ready and keeping ready.

"He is coming soon"; there is no doubt about it. Are you ready to meet Him? Do you want Him to come soon? If your life has been placed in God's hands, if you have accepted Jesus Christ as your Saviour, then you will recognize Him as the promised Deliverer who comes to rescue you from an alien world of sin to make you a part of His kingdom of glory. When this truth really dawns on your heart, you will be able to say with Martin Luther, "May the Lord Jesus come at once! Let Him cut the whole matter short with the day of judgment; for there is no amendment to be expected." Your heart will beat sympathetically with the English reformer and martyr Ridley, who wrote, "The world, without doubt—this I do believe, and therefore say it—draws toward an end. Let us with John, the servant of God, cry in our hearts unto our Saviour, Christ, 'Come, Lord Jesus, come!'"

COMMITTED TO HIS COMING

AS A BOY I sincerely believed that Jesus Christ was coming again to this world, literally and soon. My parents accepted this devoutly, and they spoke of it often in our home. In our little church this doctrine was preached often, and in my Sabbath School class it was frequently discussed. So real did the coming of the Lord become to me, and so impressed was I of its nearness, that I frequently talked about it easily and unashamedly.

I attended public school about three blocks from our house, and because I went home for lunch, I walked the short distance four times each day. I can still remember the conversations during some of those walks with the unchurched boys and girls my age. Particularly well I remember the day I very earnestly told my friends about the scripture which says, "This generation shall not pass away, till all be fulfilled." Luke 21:32. I explained that these words were spoken by Christ regarding His second advent, and that He talked of the generation which would see certain things taking place on the earth.

I was convinced that those signs were taking place in the world about us then, and that it would be our generation which would live to see the fulfillment of all things in the coming of the

Lord in the clouds of heaven. Very vividly I can recall describing the coming of the Lord as we walked slowly along the street toward school. Pointing to the sky, I assured a schoolmate that one of these days we would see a cloud about the size of a man's hand. This cloud would grow larger as it approached the earth, and finally we would see Jesus literally, in person, seated as it were upon the cloud, coming as King of kings and Lord of lords.

And I recall that the children with whom I talked listened most attentively. It was all very real to me then because it had been real to those who had told me of it. Children are indeed impressionable!

That was more than thirty years ago, and now I am an adult. Experience has taught me a great deal, of course. I have a better understanding of life now than I did then. I now have a knowledge of history and the sciences and philosophy about which I knew practically nothing then. I can see man's place in the scheme of things to a much better degree. I hope I am not as naïve or impressionable now as when I was a child. I am sure I weigh things more carefully, and I believe I am better equipped to evaluate the things that I am taught. I have been fooled a number of times in my life, and this has made me more cautious about what I accept. I have come to realize, because I have seen it so many times, that even sincere people can be badly misguided.

So, with maturity and experience, how do I feel thirty years later about Christ's second coming? How has my increased knowledge and understanding affected the earnest belief of my childhood? I now believe in Christ's literal, imminent second coming even more than ever!

But my trust now is not the credulity of a naïve child. Rather, it is the considered judgment of what I hope is a mature man. My belief in the advent of our Lord, of course, has been assailed in the intervening years, and as a result I now am acquainted with the cons as well as the pros. I have talked many times with unbelievers as well as with believers. I have studied under doubters in a university, as well as under Christian believers in a seminary; but despite all this, *I believe*—and believe now more than ever.

I shall never forget the exhilarating thrill which filled my soul one sultry Sabbath afternoon as alone I made my ascent up the ancient slopes of the Mount of Olives in the old land of Jordan. I had never dared dream, in my wildest days of imagination and anticipation, that such an opportunity would ever be mine. I took in all that was to be seen as I happily continued my climb. The Garden of Gethsemane was now below me and at my left. All about me were graves of believers of past centuries who wished to be interred in this sacred area.

Finally I reached the summit, lost in awe and reverie as I pictured the hallowed scene which took place nineteen hundred years ago when the Lord Jesus Christ arose from the earth right near this spot and ascended into heaven. My heart beat faster as I realized it was right here that angel messengers had approached the bewildered, watching disciples with the words, "Ye men of Galilee, why stand ye gazing up into heaven? this same Jesus, which is taken up from you into heaven, shall so come in like manner as ye have seen him go into heaven." Acts 1:11. And I stared up into the cloudless sky that afternoon with those words ringing in my mind's ear and tried to imagine what it must have been like to "have seen him go."

But then my mind went forward to what it will be like to see Him come again, for I remembered that the Scriptures teach that His feet will ultimately touch earth again upon the summit of the Mount of Olives. (Zechariah 14:4.) This verse teaches also that this mount will divide in two, forming "a very great valley," thus providing a place for the Holy City, the New Jerusalem, which descends from God in heaven to this earth. And that also was quite an event for me to picture.

From looking up and down, backward and forward in time, I turned and viewed the city of Jerusalem. Almost instantly I remembered what Luke tells us happened when Jesus stood on the very spot where I now stood and took in the scene which so moved me. "And when he was come near, he beheld the city, and wept over it, saying, If thou hadst known, even thou, at least in this thy day, the things which belong unto thy peace! but now they are hid from thine eyes. For the days shall come upon thee, that thine enemies shall cast a trench about thee, and compass thee round, and keep thee in on every side, and shall lay thee even with the ground, and thy children within thee; and they shall not leave in thee one stone upon another; because thou knewest not the time of thy visitation." Luke 19:41-44.

Christ's prophetic words were literally and terribly fulfilled. Jerusalem was destroyed, and the beautiful Temple of which the Jewish people were so proud was laid waste. Upon the spot where the Temple once was, a Muslim mosque now stands. All evidences of the former glory are gone.

But to the disciples it seemed as if the destruction of Jerusalem could be equated only with the destruction of the entire earth at the end of all things. Therefore they inquired, "Tell us, when shall these things be? and what shall be the sign of thy coming, and of the end of the world?" Matthew 24:3. In the conversation which followed, Jesus indicated that the destruction of Jerusalem would not be the end of all things. He then spoke of the fact that He would come again and related for them many signs which would indicate when the time of His advent was approaching.

Jesus made it clear on a number of occasions that He was coming again to this earth. It is impossible to believe His words and not believe in His second coming, for He said, "Let not your heart be troubled: ye believe in God, believe also in me. In my Father's house are many mansions: if it were not so, I would have told you. I go to prepare a place for you. And if I go and prepare a place for you, I will come again, and receive you unto myself; that where I am, there ye may be also." John 14:1-3. He is coming again, literally. And the angels said that "this same Jesus" is coming again "as ye have seen him go into heaven."

I have changed my views on many things in the past thirty years, for experience has brought understanding. But the understanding of my maturity has served only to strengthen my confidence in the coming of my Lord. The years have never given me any reason not to believe in the second coming of Jesus. Rather, they have given me abundant reason to be glad for my faith, "the blessed hope."

Not long ago I drove up the shady gravel road which leads into a little cemetery in my hometown in upstate New York. It was not difficult for me to find the little spot I sought. Many times as a child I had come to this family plot with my grandmother, who now lies buried there. In the center of the plot is a large stone bearing my family name, and around it are smaller stones containing the names of various members of my family. Uncles, aunts, grandparents—I knew every one of them well, except my grandfather who died before I was born.

But one grave there means more to me than the rest. It is the grave of my father. My other relatives did not have his hope or his faith. As I stood looking upon his grave, I thought of all he had taught me, and of how much his faith in the second coming of Jesus Christ had meant to him. I remembered the long period of his illness, when he knew that life was going to be short for him and that at a premature age he would die. He talked often then, even more than usual, about the second coming of Jesus. He encouraged us to make plans for caring for family matters which he would not be able to attend to. But over and beyond all of that, he looked forward to the day of reunion when he hoped to see us all again.

I recalled the morning I received the telephone message that during the night life had slipped away from him. Somehow that day I could not imagine a world without my father. I could not dream of what it would be like to face my problems without being able to discuss them with him.

In the following two or three days, as I gradually accepted the idea that he was gone, I experienced a new dedication. I resolved that by God's grace I was going to be faithful to Him and meet my father on that resurrection morning. Therefore my belief in the second coming of Jesus is not merely a theological doctrine to which I have given mental assent. Rather, it is very real to me—as real as meeting my own father again. It is as real as living—but living forever without grief, loss, or pain.

Natives in the Fiji Islands have a pathetic custom of calling out after their dead loved ones. The mourner climbs a high tree or cliff, shouting his dead friend's name and crying, "Come back! Come back!" But all the calls in the world, from the most prominent places of earth, will not bring back the dead. The wind simply throws the cry back in the caller's face.

But Christians who stand by the gravesides of our Christian dead know that they will come back when our Lord returns the second time to this earth. We cling to the resurrection promise: "I would not have you to be ignorant, brethren, concerning them which are asleep, that ye sorrow not, even as others which have no hope. For if we believe that Jesus died and rose again, even so them also which sleep in Jesus will God bring with him. . . . For the Lord himself shall descend from heaven with a shout, with the voice of the archangel, and with the trump of God: and the dead in Christ shall rise first: then we which are alive and remain shall be caught up together with them in the clouds, to meet the Lord in the air: and so shall we ever be with the Lord." 1 Thessalonians 4:13-17.

Many years ago the aged Apostle Paul wrote to his beloved friend Timothy, whom he called his son in the faith, this admonition: "Continue thou in the things which thou hast learned and hast been assured of, knowing of whom thou hast learned them; and that from a child thou hast known the holy scriptures, which are able to make thee wise unto salvation through faith which is in Christ Jesus." 2 Timothy 3:14, 15. "O Timothy, keep that which is committed to thy trust, avoiding profane and vain babblings, and oppositions of science falsely so called." 1 Timothy 6:20.

To me also, like Timothy, was "committed" as a child the belief in the second coming of our Lord. I have kept it ever in my heart since that day. By God's grace I will "continue . . . in the things" which I have learned and have "been assured of," certain that the Holy Scriptures are able to make any man "wise unto salvation through faith . . . in Christ Jesus."

THE
SINNER'S
PUNISHMENT

RECENTLY a prominent bishop startled a great number of religious people when he declared his conclusion that many historic doctrines of the church are actually no more than primitive religious myths. Asked to name a few, he included Adam and Eve in the Garden of Eden and "the existence of a sky-high heaven and a red-hot hell." As I read his views in the newspaper one morning, I was as surprised as anyone, for in order to counteract the effect of the Scriptures' teachings, he even felt it necessary to undermine faith in them, saying he believed the Bible came about as "a sort of *Reader's Digest* anthology."

But perhaps I was even more startled a little later when the results of a survey provoked by the announcement of the bishop's views were published. Louis Harris and Associates, a distinguished public opinion research firm, interviewed a scientific sampling of young divinity students who will soon provide spiritual leadership for the sixty-five million churchgoing Protestants in the United States. They were assigned to find out what these ministers of tomorrow believe about the bishop's views.

Probably everyone was surprised at how much the young ministerial students agreed with the bishop. Only 29 percent, a little more than a quarter of them, stated a belief in a real heaven and a real hell. As I reflected on this, I could not help wondering why there is a mass rejection of what our fathers considered essential and basic religious beliefs. I believe I have correctly concluded that many have rejected not so much the doctrines of the Bible, but rather what men have done to these doctrines. Because some do not understand, they think the Bible teaches something it does not.

Take, for instance, the "red-hot hell" rejected by so many of today's and tomorrow's theologians. What an abundance of misunderstanding exists in the world on this subject! Several years ago this was brought rather forcibly to my attention.

I was visiting in a home where the mother and the children were members of my church. The husband and father suddenly spoke vehemently to me on why he had completely rejected all religious belief and practice after being reared in a Christian home. With truly deep conviction he exploded, "I wouldn't catch the worst poisonous snake and then roast him alive in a barbecue pit in my backyard. I could get no enjoyment out of it, for I don't get pleasure out of seeing anything in agony. I would have enough heart to put it out of its misery. But your God must be a sadistic fiend! He roasts not snakes, but *people,* alive in the fires of hell—eternally—and deliberately uses His power to keep them alive in order to hear them scream. Then He laughs derisively in their faces at their suffering." With a curse he added, "If that is your kind of God, I hate Him."

In the following months I grew to know that man fairly well, and happily I was able to help him with his point of view about God—for my God is not at all the kind of God he had pictured. But many, like that man, have rejected not only the red-hot hell but even God Himself because of misunderstanding on this point. Therefore the subject deserves careful consideration.

I must admit that I have never enjoyed being punished for wrongdoing. Probably you feel the same. Neither do I enjoy seeing someone else punished, even though I might know he richly deserves it. Are you, too, as "softhearted" as this? Then remember that God is infinitely more compassionate and tender-hearted than you and I ever thought of being. He even tells us that His entire character can be equated with love. Of Himself He says, "God is love." How then, you ask, could He be guilty of the things that men say He will do to the wicked? In fact, why must there be any such thing as a future punishment for evildoers? A little thought might make the matter clearer.

Would you want a world in which everything was all right to do, as long as a man did not get caught? Would you want a world in which "might makes right," with "Truth forever on the scaffold, Wrong forever on the throne"? When you stop and think about it, you realize that God must be more than just a God of love and kindness—or perhaps it would be more proper to say that His love and kindness must not prevent Him from being completely fair and just. All of us must be able to know that He as our heavenly Father and the Ruler of all will see to it that matters in the world about us ultimately work out as they should.

To be even more specific, I must be able to know that it is not necessary for me to seek vengeance and redress for the unpunished grievances of my life. I must know that God is keeping score for me and that I can safely leave everything to Him who has said, "Vengeance is mine; I will repay, saith the Lord." Romans 12:19. I must have the certainty that in the world ruled by Him men will receive what they give, will reap what they sow—if not now, then later. This is the reason behind the almost stern warnings against wrongdoing to be found in the Scriptures. And when I stop and think about it, I must confess I would not have it otherwise.

I have heard of parents who have told their children when punishing them, "This hurts me more than it does you." I am not sure that is always the case. But with God I feel it is correct. He does not want to punish. His plea to us all is to turn from our evil ways and live. "As I live, saith the Lord God, I have no pleasure in the death of the wicked; but that the wicked turn from his way and live: turn ye, turn ye from your evil ways; for why will ye die, O house of Israel?" Ezekiel 33:11. Like a wise and good parent, He must let His children know that good will ultimately receive its reward and that evil will surely reap its penalty.

But after having agreed to that, we come more directly to the area of general misunderstanding. How will God punish the wicked, and for how long? The ancient pagans conceived of an underground place where evildoers went after death for a period of regeneration. Unfortunately, the early Christian church rather quickly drifted into apostasy and adopted many of the teachings and outlooks of paganism. This idea of the fate of the wicked manifested itself in the Christian church in the early centuries, and out of it came the concepts of limbo, purgatory, and an ever-burning hell.

Now let me perhaps startle you with a statement of fact which might appear to be bold and even brash. *According to the Bible not a single soul is burning in the fires of hell at present.* Here is a Scriptural reference to prove it, in the words of Jesus Himself: "As therefore the tares are gathered and burned in the fire; so shall it be in the end of this world. The Son of man shall send forth his angels, and they shall gather out of his kingdom all things that offend, and them which do iniquity, and shall cast them into a furnace of fire: there shall be wailing and gnashing of teeth." Matthew 13:40-42.

The wicked, then, will be punished at the end of this world, at the second coming of Jesus Christ. Nothing could be clearer. Peter teaches that the wicked are being *reserved* until the day of judgment to be punished. "The Lord knoweth how to deliver the godly out of temptations, and to reserve the unjust unto the day of judgment to be punished." 2 Peter 2:9. And that makes sense. Surely God would not punish a man before he went to judgment.

The Bible also teaches that the wicked will be raised from the dead before they are punished. "But the fearful, and unbelieving, and the abominable, and murderers, and whoremongers, and sorcerers, and idolaters, and all liars, shall have their part in the lake which burneth with fire and brimstone: which is the second death." Revelation 21:8. If this punishment of hellfire results in the second death, the wicked must have been raised from their first death.

Do you know where the hell of the Bible is located? Did you ever hear anyone say? Many carry the vague notion, which had its inception in paganism, that hell is located somewhere underground, perhaps in the middle of the earth. But the Bible certainly does not teach this. It says, "Behold, the righteous shall be recompensed in the earth: much more the wicked and the sinner." Proverbs 11:31. This earth, then, is to be the place where the wicked will receive their punishment. And again perfect uniformity prevails among the Bible writers on this subject. Peter tells us, "The earth also and the works that are therein shall be burned up." Then he adds, "Nevertheless we, according to his promise, look for new heavens and a new earth, wherein dwelleth righteousness." 2 Peter 3:10, 13.

In Revelation 20 we are given in sequence the events which will finally result in the destruction of the wicked upon this earth. Here we are told that ultimately God's Holy City, called the New Jerusalem, will descend to this earth. The wicked will then be resurrected and will surround the city, attempting to capture it. They will be led by Satan, who is making one final effort to fight against God. But at the height of their rebellion Heaven puts an end to it all. "And they went up on the breadth of the earth, and compassed the camp of the saints about, and the beloved city: and fire came down from God out of heaven, and devoured them." Revelation 20:9. This is what is commonly referred to as hellfire.

Now we come to another area of great misunderstanding. What will this fire do to the wicked? Read these plain teachings from God's Word: "For, behold, the day cometh, that shall burn as an oven; and all the proud, yea, and all that do wickedly, shall be stubble: and the day that cometh shall burn them up, saith the Lord of hosts, that it shall leave them neither root nor branch. . . . And ye shall tread down the wicked; for they shall be ashes under the soles of your feet in the day that I shall do this, saith the Lord of hosts." Malachi 4:1-3. How can these words be misunderstood? Plainly they tell us that the wicked will be reduced to ashes. For them this will be the "second *death*."

The psalmist also makes the matter very clear in the words, "For yet a little while, and the wicked shall not be: yea, thou shalt diligently consider his place, and it shall not be." "But the wicked shall perish: . . . they shall consume; into smoke shall they consume away." Psalm 37:10, 20. These words do not teach an ever-burning hell with eternal torture.

Rather, they teach that the time will come when the wicked will no longer exist. They state that even diligent searching for the place of the wicked—hell—will reveal only that it exists no more. The fires will have done their work and gone out. All through the Bible words and expressions like these are applied to the wicked: "shall die," "perish," "melt away," "fade away," "wither," "be as nothing," "be no more," "be destroyed," "consumed utterly," "cut asunder." And there are others equally strong.

The Bible teaches that "the wages of sin is *death*; but the gift of God is eternal life through Jesus Christ our Lord." (Romans 6:23.) The contrast is between eternal death and eternal life, not eternal life in both cases with suffering for the one and bliss for the other. The favorite Bible text of many, John 3:16, says, "For God so loved the world, that he gave his only begotten Son, that whosoever believeth in him should not perish, but have everlasting life." Only the righteous, those who accept Jesus Christ, are to have everlasting life. The fate of the wicked is to "perish."

Some texts of Scripture might prove difficult to understand; but if one will study them in the light of these verses, looking for their deeper meaning, he will discover that the scriptures on this subject as on all others are perfectly harmonious. When God speaks of everlasting punishment, it is not hard to understand what is meant if one remembers that death is the punishment and that it will indeed be everlasting.

God, then, will punish the wicked, but He will punish them in keeping with His own justice and love. He calls it His "strange act," because it is so contrary to the long-suffering and mercy He has always bestowed on the human family. He will mercifully destroy those who would not want to live eternally in His presence.

A Christian minister talked one day to a man about giving his heart to the Lord Jesus. Rather flippantly the man replied, "Don't trouble yourself about me, sir. I'll slip into heaven with the crowd someday." After a thoughtful moment the minister answered, "My friend, you have mistaken the place, for if you slip in with the crowd, you will slip into hell. The Scriptures say, 'Wide is the gate, and broad is the way, that leadeth to destruction, and many there be which go in thereat: because strait is the gate, and narrow is the way, which leadeth unto life, and few there be that find it.'" Matthew 7:13, 14.

Which way are you going? Are you slipping in with the crowd, following the path of least resistance? or are you attempting to find a place in God's kingdom with the redeemed? To accomplish that you must be willing to stand alone if need be. Jesus died for you in order that you might not perish, but have everlasting life. Will you not accept the eternal life He offers? You will never be sorry that you did.

GOD'S
FINAL
JUDGMENT

HAVE YOU ever received a summons ordering you to appear in court on a certain day? How did you feel about it? Did you dread the whole idea?

Very few people react with any joy on such an occasion, and many have a similar reaction when hearing that before any of us reach God's kingdom "we must all appear before the judgment seat of Christ." (2 Corinthians 5:10.) Indeed many feel sympathetic with Felix who "trembled" when Paul reasoned with him of "judgment to come." But why do we feel this way about courts of law? And should we Christians dread God's final judgment?

Perhaps our apprehension is due to a feeling of unsureness whether we will receive a sympathetic hearing. I learned this the hard way as a boy in the eighth grade.

In the school I attended, a debating team had been formed which was the pride and joy of Mr. Porter, the principal, who personally directed all of its activities. There was nothing to which I aspired more at the moment than a place on that team. When it was announced at the beginning of the school year that anyone wishing to participate with the debating team should write a paper on the subject of the first debate and submit it to the principal, I enthusiastically began my preparation.

I can still remember how long, hard, and earnestly I worked on that paper on which rested my boyish hopes. After it was completed, I feared that because it was not typed it might not receive all the attention I hoped it deserved. Since typing was a skill I had not had opportunity to cultivate, I prevailed upon an older cousin of mine to copy it for me.

At the appointed hour I laid it on the principal's desk along with the rest. A quick glance at the others revealed that mine obviously was the finest in appearance. The days that followed were a bit hard for me to live through as I anxiously awaited word as to whether or not I had made the team.

A few days later I was summoned to Mr. Porter's office for a personal interview. I remember him as being a rather stern man with gray hair and a sharp, crisp way of speaking, which made all of us regard him with great respect.

As I moved about uneasily in my chair, Mr. Porter began by praising highly the thoughts and arguments presented in my paper. But he followed this by telling me that he would have to select others for the coveted places on the team. He seemed to be saying something else, the full meaning of which I did not immediately grasp. Finally he queried, "Who typed your paper for you? Surely you did not do it yourself, did you?" When I informed him that a cousin had done this, our brief interview came to an abrupt end.

I left his office crestfallen. But as I made my way down the corridor, the awful truth of what he had been trying to say suddenly dawned upon me. He had concluded that not only had someone else *typed* my paper, but someone else also had *written* it! And on that basis he had barred me from the team. Deeply humiliated, I had no idea how to cope with the injustice of the situation. As a result, I said and did nothing in my own defense.

A year later when another debating team was organized in the same way, I not only was chosen as a member, but was made captain of the team. This should, in a measure, have compensated for the unpleasantness and hurt of the year before, but to this day I cannot remember anything about the debates we gave or the trips we took to other schools to meet opposing teams. Neither can I recall the victories or defeats, nor even the subjects upon which we debated. All that remains is the memory of the bitter suffering over being disqualified because of a crime I had not committed. Human beings who have to form opinions on outward appearances can be entirely wrong in their judgments. And this can happen in a court of law also—reason enough to give some feelings of foreboding about receiving a summons to appear before a judge.

I once visited a young man on Death Row who had been convicted of killing his estranged wife as they sat alone in the family car. Constantly and to the end he protested his innocence, claiming that when his wife became convinced they could never reestablish their home, she in despair had committed suicide in his presence. The jury did not believe his story, and the judge sentenced him to death.

But one of his guards who had lived with him for the months he spent behind bars told me privately that he was absolutely convinced that the young man was telling the truth. A few days after this visit, however, he died in the electric chair for allegedly killing his wife. Because of my knowledge I shall always feel that an injustice was done. Men in their finite judgments can make mistakes, and even the innocent may on occasion have reason to dread a summons.

Sometimes a law itself is unjust. Not long ago I stood before a magistrate with a man whom the clerk of the court announced was charged with "Sabbathbreaking." He had been arrested for working on Sunday and, incidentally, for doing religious work on Sunday at that. To me such a law is unjust, and I am happy that attempts are being made to have it repealed. The Sabbath is a wholly religious institution, and in my opinion no one should attempt to legislate on religious matters.

But we have no reason to fear to stand before God's great tribunal for any reasons like these. We can take comfort in the fact that we have the best Attorney we could ever secure, One truly interested in our case. As a matter of fact, our Advocate is also our Saviour, who loved us enough to give His life for us on Calvary. The Scriptures tell us, "If any man sin, we have an advocate with the Father, Jesus Christ the righteous." 1 John 2:1.

The Greek word here translated "advocate," *paraklētos,* does not mean a lawyer in the judicial sense of the term. If it did, some might have reason to conclude that God is a stern and cruel judge, who is going to be exacting in His dealings with us. Under such circumstances it may be thought that we need someone to plead our case to prevent God from being too harsh with us. Such is not the case.

God is as merciful, kind, and interested in our salvation as is Christ. Jesus once explained, "He that hath seen me hath seen the Father." God and Christ are one, working in the fullest cooperation for the salvation of man. Satan has attempted to twist our ideas of the character of God to make us think we need someone to intercede for us with an unwilling God who is eager to destroy us. Nothing could be farther from the truth. The Bible tells us that Jesus, our Mediator, or Go-between, does not have to overcome God's reluctance to save us; He merely takes hold of God's willingness, pleading His shed blood to cover all of our confessed sins.

Furthermore, not only is Jesus our Advocate, but He serves in the unprecedented dual role of advocate and judge. To me this is one of the most heartening truths of the Scriptures. In John 5:22, 27 we are told, "For the Father judgeth no man, but hath committed all judgment unto the Son," "and hath given him authority to execute judgment also, because he is the Son of man."

When we realize that the One who will finally judge us is none other than Jesus Christ, the One who would have gone to Calvary had there been only one person needing salvation, we can grasp the fact that this will be a most unusual court, one in which everything will be done to save the individuals to be judged.

And we need not fear being misunderstood or lacking the ability to express ourselves properly in God's court. An accurate record of our lives has been kept by angel scribes, and these unerring books are used as the basis of testimony. "And the books were opened: and another book was opened, which is the book of life: and the dead were judged out of those things which were written in the books, according to their works." Revelation 20:12. No chance of mistakes or misunderstanding here.

I have always found special encouragement in the words recorded in Revelation 3:5: "He that overcometh, the same shall be clothed in white raiment; and I will not blot out his name out of the book of life, but I will confess his name before my Father, and before his angels."

None of us is perfect, and if in the judgment the angels read only the sordid and sorry record of our unfortunate lives, then there could be no hope for any of us. I do not like to think of how I would feel on hearing such a recital. But the promise of salvation is not made to perfect and sinless ones, for no such individuals exist in all the world. Rather, the promise is for the *overcomers*—men who have fallen into sin, but who have been forgiven as their sins are washed away in the blood of the Lamb, and who have gone on to overcome. In the strength of Christ, that can include you and me. *I* can be an overcomer. *I* can accept the help that He so freely offers. So can *you*.

Besides being our Judge and our Advocate, Jesus is also our Intercessor, the great High Priest of all who claim His righteousness. If we have accepted Him as our Lord and Saviour, He will confess before God and all the holy angels in that day of judgment that He knows us to be His loyal and devoted followers. He has promised not to blot our names out of the book of life, even though this is what we deserve for our sins. He who paid the price for our sins on Calvary proudly admits before the universe that we are His and He is ours, and that the ransom price He paid was for us.

This, then, is indeed a very unusual court—one in which everything possible has been done to ensure a favorable decision for the accused.

In a way the relationship between ourselves and God is more closely related to a family situation than to a court of law. Let me try to explain it as I see it.

Let us suppose that a certain father has two sons, the younger of whom tends to be very willful. His father warns him repeatedly that his wrong day-by-day choices will end in ultimate catastrophe, but all his warnings seem to fall on deaf ears. Finally in a rebellious burst of self-will, the younger son goes "off the deep end" and brings disgrace upon the family name, thus alienating himself from the rest.

Let us now suppose that the older brother decides to attempt to reunite all in understanding and forgiveness. His first work must be not with the father, but with the brother, attempting to change his attitude, causing him to feel sorry for his wrongdoing, and attempting to lead him to a change of heart. Only after this has been fully accomplished does he go to the father, telling him of his brother's repentance. He does not need to attempt to get the father to love his son again—the father has loved him all along. He seeks only to make father and son at one again.

This work as a go-between is that done for all of us by Jesus, our Elder Brother, and the work accomplished for us is called the "atonement," truly an at-one-ment. What a wonderful relationship is this! With Christ, my Elder Brother, pleading my case, I have no reason to fear having my name come before the God of the universe, who is also my heavenly Father. He has loved me all along and wants me saved.

And the law which we must face and with which our lives will be compared, is not unjust, as are some laws. It is God's great Ten Commandment law. James refers to this law in these words: "So speak ye, and so do, as they that shall be judged by the law of liberty." James 2:12. This law, if obeyed, brings liberty of spirit to all.

And yet while emphasizing that God's judgment will be filled with the understanding which a tender and ideal father and a loving and self-sacrificing elder brother have for a wayward son, it would be wrong to infer that this gives any of us license to trifle with God's commands. The finest of parents are those who expect obedience to the family's rules. Even so God expects His children to obey Him. A happy, harmonious family relationship does not exist when one member insists upon being willful, pursuing his own independent course of action.

Surely no one would deliberately choose a life of willful disobedience and expect God to overlook this in the day of judgment. We have been told, "For God shall bring every work into judgment, with every secret thing, whether it be good, or whether it be evil." Ecclesiastes 12:14. Those who choose disobedience choose the everlasting punishment of the second death. "And these shall go away into everlasting punishment: but the righteous into life eternal." Matthew 25:46. How much better to choose the life eternal made possible through Christ, who "became the author of eternal salvation unto all them that obey him"! (Hebrews 5:9.)

Prophecy discloses that in the last days of earth's history a special judgment-hour message is to go to the world. John the revelator pictured an angel flying through heaven preaching the everlasting gospel to all who dwell on the earth and "saying with a loud voice, Fear God, and give glory to him; for the hour of his judgment is come: and worship him that made heaven, and earth, and the sea, and the fountains of waters." (Revelation 14:7.) In view of the arrival of God's judgment hour, all men are called upon to fear or reverence God and give glory to Him. They are called upon to give Him the worship due His name. Such service is a privilege.

The Bible makes it abundantly clear that today's judgment-bound generation need fear its day in heaven's court only as it fails to comply with God's laws. The individual who has truly glorified God by a program of consistent Christian living need not be concerned about the penalties meted out in the great day of judgment.

So I do not fear the judgment. Why should I? I have, through Christ, cared for my sins already in that I have accepted Him as my Saviour and Lord. "Some men's sins are open beforehand, going before to judgment; and some men they follow after." 1 Timothy 5:24. Jesus is my Advocate, my Judge, my Elder Brother, my Intercessor. God is my loving heavenly Father who understands. They both want to see me saved. Christ died to make it possible. I have only to choose to follow Him. Because of all this I have nothing to fear. Can you say the same?

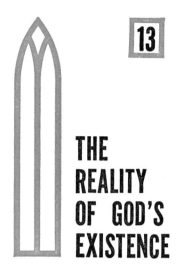

THE
REALITY
OF GOD'S
EXISTENCE

DO YOU BELIEVE that God exists? Do you *really* believe it—enough to risk a part of your income on His promise to take a personal hand in your affairs? Permit me to explain before you answer.

I used to live near the Niagara Falls, and despite frequent visits I never quite got over my awe of the mighty force of the hurtling waters. But to me, as awesome as the falls themselves are the whirlpool rapids downstream in the Niagara River. Many are the tales about men and women who have drowned as they were unable to escape the terrible grip of those powerful whirlpools. I could never look at those troubled, circling waters without remembering a story I heard my father tell when I was a boy.

It seems that at one time a brave and perhaps foolhardy tightrope walker announced his intention to walk to the opposite shore on a cable stretched across those treacherous rapids. To make the feat even more challenging, he further announced that he would push a wheelbarrow across before him. A large and excited crowd gathered at the appointed time and place on the Niagara River, and the tension became great when the daring performer ascended to a platform from which he would begin his hazardous journey.

Turning to the crowd, he asked if they really believed he would make it safely to the other side. At first no one wanted to commit himself, but finally a man broke the silence, expressing his faith in the performer's ability. In answer to repeated questions he affirmed with great conviction his certainty that the crossing would be made safely. With a grin the tightrope artist then replied, "All right; if you believe I will get across safely, come up here and ride across in the wheelbarrow." Such a challenge made a real difference. His faith failed the acid test, which led the laughing crowd to conclude that he never had really believed. And perhaps they were right.

I therefore ask again, Do you really believe that God exists? Do you believe it enough to get into the wheelbarrow? Take a good look at the wheelbarrow and the rapids before committing yourself. Here is the acid test put in very practical terms: Do you believe strongly enough in the existence of God to be willing to test His promises by returning 10 percent of your income—a tithe—to His work as He has requested, in full expectation that He will keep His promise and make the nine tenths you have left go farther than the ten tenths would have gone?

If you believe that an all-powerful God exists, you should believe that He *could* do this. And if you believe He exists, then surely you believe that He keeps His promises. If you hesitate to return the tenth to Him, is this not an indication that basically you do not really believe God exists or that you do not really believe He keeps His promises? Your unwillingness to get into the wheelbarrow indicates something is seriously wrong with your faith.

But perhaps you never knew until now that God requires a tenth of our increase. Here is what He says: "Will a man rob God? Yet ye have robbed me. But ye say, Wherein have we robbed thee? In tithes and offerings. Ye are cursed with a curse: for ye have robbed me, even this whole nation. Bring ye all the tithes into the storehouse, that there may be meat in mine house, and prove me now herewith, saith the Lord of hosts, if I will not open you the windows of heaven, and pour you out a blessing, that there shall not be room enough to receive it. And I will rebuke the devourer for your sakes, and he shall not destroy the fruits of your ground; neither shall your vine cast her fruit before the time in the field, saith the Lord of hosts." Malachi 3:8-11.

This is quite a dramatic and all-inclusive promise, a promise of a blessing so great that there will not be room enough in our poor lives to receive all of it, a promise to rebuke the devourer for our sakes and leave our harvests untouched by the blights which affect others about us. Translated into any economy and any age, this is a tremendous promise and challenge—a promise of God's care and blessing upon the material things of our lives if we trust Him enough to give Him a tenth of our income. Is it a promise that God keeps? Every faithful tithepayer can testify along with me that God's pledged word has not been broken.

Never shall I forget my real test on this matter. Although I had been taught from childhood to give God one penny out of every ten I received, and had done so, a real testing time came in my life when I had to decide whether I believed in God enough to get into the wheelbarrow. I have never regretted my decision.

I attended college in New England during the great depression. I started my senior year in the fall of 1938. My parents had helped me all they could, but their meager funds had dwindled and run out, and because gainful employment was so scarce, nothing was left for my college expenses. I started my senior year in debt, owing the college $125 from the previous year. That does not sound like much in this period of easy money and inflated dollars, but it was equivalent to almost $400 today, and I was faced with an almost insurmountable problem. I secured employment and was delighted to find that if I could keep my health and work the hours that I planned, I could have all the time I needed for my studies and still earn enough to pay all my expenses and graduate with my class without owing a dollar.

In fact, this was mandatory, because college rules then were similar to college rules at present—no one was allowed to graduate if he owed the college anything. But then the disturbing thought came to me that I was making no provision for the regular payment of my tithe. Were I to give 10 percent of my income to God's work, I would never be able to make it financially. Surely God wanted me to graduate, I reasoned, for I looked forward to a place in His work. I decided that I needed some counsel from someone who understood God's requirements and had my complete trust.

The next day I saw my religion professor, a man in whom I had great confidence, walking toward me across the campus. We met under an old gnarled apple tree and stood with our feet among its fallen leaves. I have seen the spot often since. It is rather sacred to me, for it is the place where I made a vitally important decision which has profoundly influenced my life.

Kicking the leaves as I tried to find the way to phrase my problem, I asked the kindly professor for counsel. I recall concluding with the question, "Do you really think God expects me to return a tenth to Him when I'm in debt, and when doing this means that I will jeopardize the completion of my college education?"

He looked very thoughtful for a moment and then said, "Indeed you are in trouble. I had not realized before what a problem you face. Surely you need God's blessing. In fact, you need more of it than I do, because you are in debt. I don't know of any way to secure God's blessing upon your monetary resources other than to be faithful in the matter of the tithe."

I had my answer and that very moment made my decision. I feel to this day a well of gratitude in my heart that it was the right decision, and I never missed a week in returning my tithe to the work of God.

But, unfortunately, the college year that followed was just as bad as I had anticipated it might be. The problem of earning enough money was a constant worry to me. As hard as I worked, I could not pick up a cent on my indebtedness. After a time it became apparent that I would end the year owing as much as I had owed when I began. In the spring I was invited to visit with the business manager of the college, who reminded me of my financial obligation and of the rule that I would not be allowed to graduate with a debt. He asked if the school should order my cap and gown or if I intended to defer graduation. Since I was class president, my responsibility to graduate weighed heavily on me. I told the business manager to order the cap and gown and that the bill would be paid before I graduated.

But the passing weeks did not make the situation any better, and I marvel at the patience of the college officials who took me at my word, despite my inadequate resources. However, God did not forget me and my problem.

Along with the other seniors, I had invited relatives and friends to my graduation. The night before commencement all of us donned our caps and gowns and waited to enter the auditorium for the class night exercises. The others showed the pens, watches, and various gifts which they had received as graduation presents. I could not show a single thing, for I had received no watches, pens, or other items. In fact, I had expected no gifts, completely forgetting that such a custom existed.

But I had received cash gifts which the donors did not know I needed but which God knew all about. On commencement morning these cash gifts added up to $125, the exact amount I needed to graduate. One hour before commencement I walked into the business office—dressed, incidentally, in my cap and gown—and laid down the final dollar.

Graduation brought me a double joy that day—happiness at completing a major part of my education, and cheer in having the unshakable conviction that God does indeed live and that if we are faithful with Him, He will be more than faithful with us. He will open the windows of heaven and pour out the promised blessing. My heart was so full that truly there was not room enough to receive all the blessing of Heaven. Many times in the years that have followed, I have remembered the lessons of that year, and I never have been sorry that I got into the wheelbarrow. I can testify gladly, after more than twenty-five years, that God has always kept His promises to me.

Dr. A. M. Fraser summarizes the actuating spirit of the tither: "If a man pays tithes from a mercenary motive, and because he thinks it will increase his income; if he does it in a self-righteous spirit, that he may have the glory of men; if he does it in a legalistic spirit, grudgingly and of necessity, because he thinks he must, and because he is afraid of the blight that follows disobedience; if he does it out of curiosity, as a novice would play with chemicals; if he does it in a superstitious spirit, as one would pry into the occult; if he does it carelessly or perfunctorily, as one would do it quickly and be done with it, he cannot expect much of any wholesome effect in his spiritual life and character."—*The Christian and His Money,* No. 10 of the "Know Your Bible Series," Pacific Press Publishing Association, Mountain View, California.

Rather, the returning of the tithe to the Lord is a deeply spiritual matter in which I demonstrate to myself, to God, and even to the world that God and I are partners, working together. It is my way of acknowledging that God is the Sovereign Owner of all, and that I am grateful each day for the blessings that He gives me. I know that He lives, and I want to have a part in His work. He is, in turn, aware of me and wants to help me in the problems of life I meet from day to day. And so we work together, God and I, in a happy relationship which makes me constantly aware of Him, which stimulates my faith and strengthens my obedience, which helps me avoid greed, and which makes God more real to me as the days go by.

Men through the centuries have been faithful in tithe paying. In Genesis, the first book of the Bible, appears this reference from the lips of Jacob: "Of all that thou shalt give me I will surely give the tenth unto thee." Genesis 28:22. The Scriptures tell us in Hebrews 7:2 that "Abraham gave a tenth part of all." Christ approved the idea of Christians returning the tithe to Him in these words: "Ye pay tithe of mint and anise and cummin, and have omitted the weightier matters of the law, judgment, mercy, and faith: *these ought ye to have done, and not to leave the other undone.*" Matthew 23:23.

Again, God stated in Leviticus 27:30: "And all the tithe of the land, whether of the seed of the land, or of the fruit of the tree, is the Lord's: it is holy unto the Lord." Perhaps the wisest man who ever lived tells us to return our tithe to God first, before caring for any other financial obligations: "Honour the Lord with thy substance, and with the firstfruits of all thine increase." Proverbs 3:9.

Let no one think that he returns the tithe to God in order to be saved. You cannot cover a single sin with silver or gold. In this world the wealthy may be able to buy themselves out of difficulties, but this is never true when it comes to spiritual matters. "Ye were not redeemed with corruptible things, as silver and gold, from your vain conversation; . . . but with the precious blood of Christ, as of a lamb without blemish and without spot." 1 Peter 1:18, 19. But any man saved by the precious blood of Christ out of a thankful heart gladly enters into God's plan and returns to Him the tenth.

Have you accepted the redemption offered you through the blood of Christ? Do you know that He died for *you?* Do you really believe God exists? Are you willing to get into the wheelbarrow? Then do it now. You will never be sorry you did.

14

WHEN A MAN DIES

RECENTLY my work took me for a week's stay on a warm island in the heart of the Caribbean. Unfortunately, depressing poverty is almost universal there, but despite it, the people seem to maintain a cheerful outlook.

While I was there, one of the dedicated missionaries with whom I was riding one day stopped the car before the gate of a large cemetery, explaining that he would like to take me inside for a moment. It took him a few minutes to find the grave he sought, crowded in among many others marked by much more imposing stones. Finally, however, he found it—the last resting place of a fellow missionary who, four or five years before, had become ill while serving God so far from home and had quickly passed away. He translated for me the words on the little gravestone, which included a precious text of Scripture referring to the Christian's hope of resurrection. Somehow that tiny, little-noticed spot seemed almost sacred as I gazed down upon it, thinking of the sacrifice it represented. Without doubt angels guard that hallowed ground.

Within the space of half an hour I saw ten groups of people enter that cemetery on foot, following either a horse-drawn or a motor-driven hearse bearing the body of a loved one. I was tremendously sobered to note that eight out of the ten coffins were little white fragile boxes measuring only two to three feet in length. Infant and child mortality in this area is fearfully high.

One scene seemed particularly pathetic. A little mother, with her brood of six children around her, stopped behind the hearse carrying one of those little boxes. A small grave had been dug right in the roadway to receive the body of the little child—a custom, I was told, followed by those who lack means to buy a grave. An old gravedigger stepped up quickly and literally hurled the little white coffin off the wagon-hearse and down upon the ground; then he dropped it with a sickening thud into the shallow, irregularly dug hole in the road.

No flowers were there to represent anyone's sympathy, and no friends or relatives were present to give strength to that little mother in this difficult hour. No priest, minister, or rabbi was present to conduct a religious service of any kind. The little mother sobbed quietly—dry, tired sobs—as she saw and heard the rocks and dirt piled quickly on top of the body of one so precious to her. In less than two minutes it was all over, and the old gravedigger, after stamping roughly on the grave to pack in the earth, in an utterly detached manner wandered away with his shovel. The mother, as if finally realizing the futility of staying any longer by the small mound of fresh earth, took the hands of her youngest children and, beckoning to the older ones to follow, made her way slowly and sadly toward the gate and home.

It had all been terribly and completely final, devoid of any hope whatsoever. Probably the precise location of the unmarked grave in the road would quickly be forgotten. To me it seemed that the whole thing had been little better than the burial of an animal. I, too, am a parent, and everything within me reacted in sympathy with that poor mother, but the fact that we spoke different languages prevented me from saying even a word of comfort to her. Even though my heart was full of sympathy, I felt helpless, and the experience left me indescribably depressed. My heart felt like a big ball of lead which threatened to rise up into my throat at any time as I, too, left the scene.

But I did not have long to brood, for I saw, walking through the same cemetery gate, yet another group following a hearse which carried this time the body of an adult. My attention was immediately caught by this group because three men carrying Bibles led the sober procession. Turning to the folk who accompanied me, I exclaimed, "These people must be Protestants." As the group came closer and then passed us, my friends whispered, "We know some of those people. They are Seventh-day Adventists. One of the three men carrying Bibles is the local elder of one of the Adventist churches here in town." Not quite sure if it was the thing to do, and not wishing to intrude, I yet seemed drawn to follow this group of sorrowing Christians to their open grave.

As the body of their dear one was tenderly placed in the ground, I was suddenly astonished to hear everyone in the group join in singing. I could not understand the words, but I recognized the melody instantly: "God Be With You Till We Meet Again." My friends translated each line for me as it was sung. What a note of hope sounded as they sang the chorus:

> "Till we meet, till we meet,
> Till we meet at Jesus' feet,
> Till we meet, till we meet,
> God be with you till we meet again."

I could hardly control my feelings as I heard this old hymn of hope and faith and courage being sung spontaneously under such unusual circumstances. There was nothing hopeless here. They *knew* that they were going to meet again.

Then a short burial service was conducted. The one leading out read words from the Bible, and again my friends whispered translations so that I, too, could understand. He read, "The Lord himself shall descend from heaven with a shout, with the voice of the archangel, and with the trump of God: and the dead in

Christ shall rise first: then we which are alive and remain shall be caught up together with them in the clouds, to meet the Lord in the air: and so shall we ever be with the Lord." 1 Thessalonians 4:16, 17.

He read also these words: "Behold, I shew you a mystery; We shall not all sleep, but we shall all be changed, in a moment, in the twinkling of an eye, at the last trump: for the trumpet shall sound, and the dead shall be raised incorruptible, and we shall be changed." 1 Corinthians 15:51, 52.

Then, looking out earnestly upon the group gathered around that grave, the speaker said, "We know that our loved one will come forth from this grave someday. She will see again her mother, her father, her uncle, her children"—and he pointed to each one as he mentioned the person by name. As I looked into their faces, I recognized that they were sad, of course, at losing a loved one; but theirs was not the dull, hopeless sorrow which had so affected me minutes before. And, as if to prove it, before the group left the grave, they sang again. The hymn was unfamiliar to me, but the words spoke of their dear one resting in peace until the Lord Jesus comes to awaken the sleeping dead.

In a very short space of time I had had a unique opportunity to witness the difference the Christian hope makes. Those with a trust in God left the same cemetery that day with the sadness that death and separation always bring, but with a firmer resolve than ever to live faithful Christian lives so that they can be reunited with their loved ones when Jesus comes again. I was glad that day for my hope in Christ and glad for the difference that the Christian faith makes in an hour like that. I consecrated my life anew to my God, who through Jesus Christ has given us our wonderful hope.

What do Christians believe happens to man when he dies? What is this hope which makes so much difference in the hour of grief? It is based, of course, upon what the Bible teaches.

Let us now briefly consider exactly what takes place when a man draws his last breath. Read again Psalm 146:4: "His breath goeth forth, he returneth to his earth; in that very day his thoughts perish." This verse cites three things:

1. He stops breathing.

2. His body begins the process of disintegration which will finally reduce it to the earth from which original man came.

3. His thoughts cease—he is unconscious as in sleep.

According to the Bible it is just as simple as that.

But someone may think, "That is oversimplifying the matter. Does not the Bible say that something goes back to God?" Yes, it does. "Then shall the dust return to the earth as it was: and the spirit shall return unto God who gave it." Ecclesiastes 12:7. But here is where many people read something into the Scriptures that simply is not there. Great care must be exercised that we do not give this word *spirit* a meaning which the Scriptures do not give it.

The Hebrew word here translated "spirit" is *ruach*. This word appears 379 times in the Old Testament and is translated in a number of ways, such as "breath," "wind," "courage," and "anger." It is also used to denote the life principle, the seat of the emotions, the mind, the heart, and even the moral character. The almost amazing thing, in view of the popular misconception of our day, is that this word *ruach* in all of its 379 times of use is *never* used to denote an intelligent entity capable of existence apart from a physical body so far as man is concerned. Such a concept is entirely without foundation in the Bible.

Notice how this word *ruach* is used elsewhere in this same book of the Bible: "For that which befalleth the sons of men befalleth beasts; even one thing befalleth them: as the one dieth, so dieth the other; yea, they have all one breath [*ruach*]; so that a man hath no preeminence above a beast." "Who knoweth the spirit [*ruach*] of man that goeth upward, and the spirit [*ruach*] of the beast that goeth downward to the earth?" Ecclesiastes 3:19, 21.

According to these verses both men and animals have a *ruach,* with no difference seen between them. If then the *ruach,* or "spirit," of man were to become a disembodied, conscious entity at death, the *ruach* of beasts must do the same thing. But the Bible nowhere claims such a thing for man, and no Christian, to my knowledge, claims this for animals.

The *ruach* which goes back to the God who gave it is nothing more or less than the life principle, the spark of life, which God breathes into man's nostrils at his creation. This life from God, which no man, incidentally, has been able to duplicate, at death goes back to the God who gave it. He keeps it safe until the resurrection morning, when He will return it to man.

When I spent the last three hours of his life with a prisoner named Sam Tannyhill, the prison chaplain was present for a while but soon left. Bidding good-bye to the condemned man, he said cheerfully, "Remember, you don't have to fear this thing called death which will come to you tonight. In just another three hours you are going to be in heaven. Imagine it! You will see my relatives there—tonight! Give them my greetings, will you?" Sam nodded, and the chaplain left.

But that young man had studied the Bible for several hours each day for more than a year while on Death Row. And, as the result, he now had a remarkable knowledge of what the Scriptures teach. Turning to me, he said, "I know better than that. I just didn't want to argue with him tonight." A little later he continued, "Tonight, as I look at it, I'm going to go to sleep just as I have every other night. This night will probably be longer than the rest, but I realize that the next voice I hear will be the voice of Jesus waking me up." That was a wonderfully encouraging thought to him as he faced death, and his beliefs were perfectly in harmony with the Bible.

A person is not conscious of his surroundings when he is asleep. And just so, when one is sleeping the dreamless sleep of death, he knows nothing of what is taking place about him. The Scriptures go out of their way to make this plain.

The Bible makes clear that in the unconscious state of death the dead know not anything. All their emotions, such as love, hatred, and envy, are now completely suspended; they have no interest whatsoever in what goes on in this earth, for they know nothing about it. How clear are these words: "The dead praise not the Lord, neither any that go down into silence." Psalm 115:17. If the dead were in heaven, they would certainly be praising God, but this text unequivocally states that they have gone down into *silence*.

The same truth is taught in these words: "For in death there is no remembrance of thee: in the grave who shall give thee thanks?" Psalm 6:5. The dead are not remembering God and giving Him thanks for any of His blessings. They are simply asleep.

Some may wonder if the soul does not go back to God at death. Nowhere does the Bible state this. Instead it says, "The soul that sinneth, it shall die." Ezekiel 18:4. The word *soul* is often used in the Bible to denote the entire person, as in Genesis 2:7: "And the Lord God formed man of the dust of the ground, and breathed into his nostrils the breath of life; and man became a living soul." Nowhere is the soul called immortal, nor does the Bible teach that a soul carries on existence by itself.

According to the Bible, when a man dies, he stops breathing and all of his ordinary life functions cease. His "spirit," which is nothing more than the spark of life with which God made him a living being, returns to the God who gave it, to be retained until the resurrection morning. The man himself is unconscious, asleep, unaware of his surroundings and of the passage of time. His love, envy, hatred, and all other emotions are perished. He knows nothing of what is going on in this world. No conscious entity exists apart from him, carrying on a separate existence of its own. His body disintegrates back into the elements from which the original man was made—the earth itself—and in this state he awaits the call of the Life-giver, through whom only we can have eternal life.

We who believe in Jesus Christ and who have accepted Him as our Lord and Saviour can look forward to eternal life when

He calls on the resurrection morning. The Bible tells us, "He that hath the Son hath life; and he that hath not the Son of God hath not life." 1 John 5:12. We who have Christ Jesus in our hearts have hope in the face of the finality of death. We are able to look through our tears beyond present darkness and see future brightness in Christ's second coming and the reunion which will be a part of the resurrection day.

Do you have this hope? You can have it only if Christ is your Saviour, for only if you have the Son can you have life. Having Him and the hope which He brings makes all the difference in the world in how we look at death and beyond. Accept Him today and look forward to an eternity with Him and all the redeemed.

15

AFTER DEATH WHAT?

I HAVE always had a more-than-ordinary interest in Benjamin Franklin, one of the world's most versatile geniuses. I can still muster up a glow of pleasure when given an opportunity to volunteer that he and I share the same birthday.

Franklin is buried in the old cemetery of Christ Church in Philadelphia. As you look through the iron railing, you observe that the flat stone over his grave bears no trace of the epitaph which he composed for himself. His own epitaph read as follows:

> "The body of
> Benjamin Franklin, printer
> (Like the cover of an old book,
> Its contents torn out,
> And stripped of its lettering and gilding),
> Lies here food for worms.
> Yet the work itself shall not be lost,
> For it will (as he believes) appear once more
> In a new and more beautiful edition,
> Corrected and amended
> By the Author."

Franklin wanted everyone to know after his death that his confidence was in the resurrection. And what a wonderful hope the resurrection has been to Christians down through the centuries! Thinking people with a faith would find it a near impossibility to become reconciled to a world without it. Without a resurrection and eternal life, our world would be ruled by a God who gives eternity to His stones, rocks, and rivers, but gives only threescore years and ten to man, His crowning created work. He would seem to revere the inanimate more than that which lives, breathes, thinks, and is created in His own image. What kind of Father would He be thus to treasure minerals more than the men whom He has called His own children?

But the resurrection, with its subsequent hope of eternal life, brings order and reason out of what might otherwise seem to be chaotic and unreasonable. Death was not God's original plan for man, whom He created to have dominion over His rocks, rivers, and animal life. Man, by disobedience, has brought death upon himself as a natural consequence of his wrongdoing. But someday death will be no more: "The last enemy that shall be destroyed is death." 1 Corinthians 15:26. Then man will once again be restored to "the first dominion." (Micah 4:8.) God's beautiful plans, hopes, and dreams for us, His beloved children, will then be carried out eternally.

James Russell Lowell once remarked that a fitting epitaph for him would be: "Here lies that part of James Russell Lowell which hindered him from doing well." And it is true that a major physical handicap or even something relatively minor, like a poor voice or imperfect vision, has made it impossible for many a man to accomplish what he would have willed with his life. It is also true that "the desires of the flesh are against the Spirit, and the desires of the Spirit are against the flesh; for these are opposed to each other, to prevent you from doing what you would." (Galatians 5:17, R.S.V.)

But all of that will be changed at the resurrection. "So is it with the resurrection of the dead. What is sown is perishable, what is raised is imperishable. It is sown in dishonor, it is raised in glory. It is sown in weakness, it is raised in power. It is sown a physical body, it is raised a spiritual body." 1 Corinthians 15: 42-44, R.S.V. What a glorious difference! After the resurrection no bodily handicaps will hinder us from doing well. One part of us will no more war against another. The Bible points to the resurrection of the dead at the second coming of Christ as the great moment when this change will come.

Bible writers have all looked forward to that moment of change as the focal point of human history. "If a man die, shall he live again? all the days of my appointed time will I wait, till my change come." Job 14:14. Job knew that in the normal course of events death would finally claim him, just as it has all others down through history. After that he pictured himself as waiting for the resurrection. And where would he spend this waiting time? "If I wait, the grave is mine house." Job 17:13.

And how did Job picture the condition of the waiting ones? "So man lieth down, and riseth not: till the heavens be no more, they shall not awake, nor be raised out of their sleep." Job 14:12. He pictures death as a dreamless sleep, the same as every other Bible writer does, the same as Jesus Christ Himself pictured it. Jesus said, "Our friend Lazarus sleepeth; but I go, that I may awake him out of sleep. . . . Howbeit Jesus spake of his death: but they thought that he had spoken of taking of rest in sleep." John 11:11-13. The Bible records plainly that Jesus raised Lazarus from the dead.

How much conscious thought goes on during this waiting period of sleep? None! The Bible's teachings are absolutely unmistakable on this point: "His breath goeth forth, he returneth to his earth; in that very day his thoughts perish." Psalm 146:4. "For the living know that they shall die: but the dead know not any thing. . . . Also their love, and their hatred, and their envy, is now perished; neither have they any more a portion for ever in any thing that is done under the sun." Ecclesiastes 9:5, 6. The Bible even states that a man who has died knows nothing about the subsequent activities of his children. "His sons come to honour, and he knoweth it not; and they are brought low, but he perceiveth it not of them." Job 14:21. And yet despite these clear teachings of God's Word, this is not what many believe and teach in Christendom today.

I am writing these words on a beautiful Sunday afternoon in New York. This morning I did what I am sure millions of other people did—stayed in bed just a little later than usual and enjoyed the luxury of turning on the radio by the side of my bed. The voice of one of America's best-known clergymen penetrated to my consciousness. This morning's sermon was on the subject of death. His unsupported assertions startled me completely awake.

"God," he asserted, "placed immortality within you when He made you. Your body will die, but the real you will never die, for you are immortal and you are living forever right now." He did not attempt to indicate where his idea came from, and sadly I reflected that it does not come from the Bible. The Scriptures definitely declare that God "*only* hath immortality" (1 Timothy 6:16), and that men "by patient continuance in well doing seek for . . . immortality, eternal life." (Romans 2:7.) And, according to the Scriptures, we will receive this immortality at the resurrection when "this mortal *must put on* immortality." (1 Corinthians 15:53. Italics ours.)

Why should Christians preach an un-Biblical doctrine first presented by Satan in the Garden of Eden when he contradicted God and lied to Eve, saying, "Ye shall not surely die"? Why should they follow in this regard the God-denying religions of ancient antiquity and just about every heathen religion on earth? The North American Indians used to look upon the realm of death as a kind of "happy hunting ground," where each Indian will wield renewed power with perfect weapons of warfare and will enjoy all the thrills and delights of hunting for his food. The Mohammedan believes that immediately at death he will pass swiftly over a narrow and dangerous bridge spanning a great gulf, and that he will then go to the seven heavens, where eternally he will revel in sensual pleasures.

But the Scriptures nowhere teach that the rewards of heaven will be given immediately at death. How much better it is to know that eventually all of us will go together, at the same time, to meet our Redeemer in heaven, "God having provided some better thing for us, that they without us should not be made perfect." (Hebrews 11:40.)

The conducting of funeral services has always been a difficult part of my ministry—some funerals more so than others. I remember a sweet five-year-old whose troubled little life finally came to an end after much suffering. The promises of the resurrection were especially precious as I read them in front of her little white casket before her sorrowing family. After it was all over, one of the relatives who did not fully understand the Christian faith said with choked voice that he hoped the angels were taking special care of the little one, for she had been especially dependent upon her parents and this was the first time she had ever been separated from them. He was sure she would miss her parents a great deal, even as they missed her. As I pondered his statement, I realized it was a perfectly logical conclusion for him to make, based on his idea of immediate immortality.

I once knew a good and strong husband who for years bestowed tender, loving care on his frail and dependent wife. Then suddenly he died, and the wife has had a most difficult time attempting to carry on alone. Can you imagine that husband being blissfully happy in heaven while looking down on the suffering of the one whom he loves with all his heart, and who needs and misses him so much, even praying every day that her life may soon end? Heaven could not be joyful to him under such circumstances. How much better is God's plan, which simply allows him to sleep, not knowing anything of the needs and grief of his dear companion! Someday they will have a happy reunion and meet Jesus together, being made perfect at the same time in His presence.

Read thoughtfully again these tremendous words written by the Apostle Paul to the Thessalonians: "But I would not have you to be ignorant, brethren, concerning them which are asleep, that ye sorrow not, even as others which have no hope. For if we believe that Jesus died and rose again, even so them also which sleep in Jesus will God bring with him." "For the Lord himself shall descend from heaven with a shout, with the voice of the archangel, and with the trump of God: and the dead in Christ shall rise first: then we which are alive and remain shall be caught up together with them in the clouds, to meet the Lord in the air: and so shall we ever be with the Lord. Wherefore comfort one another with these words." 1 Thessalonians 4:13, 14, 16-18.

A few years ago a submarine sank off Provincetown, Massachusetts, at the end of Cape Cod. As soon as possible, divers descended to the sunken wreck. They walked about the disabled ship, endeavoring to find some signs of life within. At last they heard a gentle tapping and recognized it to be the dots and dashes of the Morse Code. The words were, "Is there hope?"

This is the constant cry of humanity. Everyone wants to know, Is there hope for us to escape? The Christian answer is, Yes, there is hope, because Jesus died and rose again. He paid the price for every sinner. He broke the power of the tomb by rising the third day and ascending to heaven, where He lives and dwells at the right hand of God the Father. Someday He is coming again to raise the dead and to take the living who believe in Him to the heavenly home He has prepared for us.

We must live for Christ so that we can have that hope in our hearts. And if God wills that we should wait for the resurrection, may we have fallen asleep in full confidence that the next voice we hear will be the voice of Jesus waking us on the eternal morning of the resurrection. Do you not want this confidence? You can have it through Christ. Accept Him as your very own Saviour, and commit your life to His care; and the certainty of this "blessed hope" can be yours.

TEN
ETERNAL
PRINCIPLES

RECENTLY while scanning a popular magazine, I suddenly came upon an article on the Ten Commandments which arrested my attention. The author said that almost every child in our country (and he might have added, in Western Civilization) has heard of these commandments by the time he is in the first grade. He further asserted that among the many formulations of religious principles expressed through the centuries, these alone are accepted by Protestants, Catholics, and Jews.

The writer then asked some penetrating questions which set me to thinking: "Just what do these laws mean to you? . . . Have the commandments become so familiar over the centuries that they are seldom considered in the modern world? Worse, have they been deliberately set aside as worthy, perhaps, but antiquated?"

I spent a little time musing about the situation which faces us as individuals. Many people agree that the principles of the Ten Commandments are eternal and right, and that we could never possibly outgrow our need of them. And yet, perhaps unconsciously, a vast number have discarded them—at least in practice. But at what a fearful price! It is still true that "they have sown the wind, and they shall reap the whirlwind." (Hosea 8:7.)

My quiet musings led me to remember a young husband and wife who sat across from me in my study not long ago, both of them weeping. I had seen one of them grow up, and could not think of them in other than affectionate, almost fatherly terms. They had married young, perhaps too young; and now two little ones were dependent upon them. The reason for the tears? Marital infidelity. And now here they sat, crushed and bewildered. It seemed to me that they were little more than children—desperately needing something that would make it possible for them to pick up the broken pieces, dry the bitter tears of disappointment and remorse, and go on again.

We found that "something" as together we talked of a Saviour who has had to forgive every one of us often. And we found it as we prayed together that the merciful Spirit of Christ might find permanent lodging in our needy lives. After they had left, a new realization came upon me that one cannot discard even a single one of God's Ten Commandments without paying a fearful price.

And as I mused, I remembered another day when I sat almost tensely by the side of a judge as an invited guest in one of New York City's juvenile courts. Because of the youth of the offenders, no reporters or ordinary witnesses are allowed when these courts are in session. The room was deliberately arranged so that it did not look like a courtroom, and the magistrate was a kind and understanding mother who had a real feeling for the teenage boys and girls brought before her.

I cannot forget one boy in particular who stood before the bench that day. His recent history of petty larceny now made it mandatory for him to be placed in a state institution of correction. He seemed so very young and unlike the hardened criminal type. He tried not to show his feelings when told the verdict. But after one agonizing moment he could not contain himself. His contorted face as he was led weeping from the courtroom

The Ten Commandments*

I

Thou shalt have no other gods before me.

II

Thou shalt not make unto thee any graven image, or any likeness of any thing that is in heaven above, or that is in the earth beneath, or that is in the water under the earth: thou shalt not bow down thyself to them, nor serve them: for I the Lord thy God am a jealous God, visiting the iniquity of the fathers upon the children unto the third and fourth generation of them that hate me; and shewing mercy unto thousands of them that love me, and keep my commandments.

III

Thou shalt not take the name of the Lord thy God in vain; for the Lord will not hold him guiltless that taketh his name in vain.

IV

Remember the sabbath day, to keep it holy. Six days shalt thou labour, and do all thy work: but the seventh day is the sabbath of the Lord thy God: in it thou shalt not do any work, thou, nor thy son, nor thy daughter, thy manservant, nor thy maidservant, nor thy cattle, nor thy stranger that is within thy gates: for in six days the Lord made heaven and earth, the sea, and all that in them is, and rested the seventh day: wherefore the Lord blessed the sabbath day, and hallowed it.

V

Honour thy father and thy mother: that thy days may be long upon the land which the Lord thy God giveth thee.

VI

Thou shalt not kill.

VII

Thou shalt not commit adultery.

VIII

Thou shalt not steal.

IX

Thou shalt not bear false witness against thy neighbour.

X

Thou shalt not covet thy neighbour's house, thou shalt not covet thy neighbour's wife, nor his manservant, nor his maidservant, nor his ox, nor his ass, nor any thing that is thy neighbour's.

Exodus 20:3-17, King James Version.

THE MORAL LAW

THE CEREMONIAL LAW

The Two Laws

THE MORAL LAW

Is called the "royal law." James 2:8.

Was spoken by God. Deuteronomy 4:12, 13.

Was written by God on tables of stone. Exodus 24:12.

Was written "with the finger of God" on stone. Exodus 31:18.

Was placed in the ark. Exodus 40:20; 1 Kings 8:9; Hebrews 9:4.

Is "perfect." Psalm 19:7.

Is to "stand fast for ever and ever." Psalm 111:7, 8.

Was not destroyed by Christ. Matthew 5:17.

Was to be magnified by Christ. Isaiah 42:21.

Gives knowledge of sin. Romans 3:20; 7:7.

THE CEREMONIAL LAW

Is called "the law . . . contained in ordinances." Ephesians 2:15.

Was spoken by Moses. Leviticus 1:1-3.

Was "the handwriting of ordinances." Colossians 2:14.

Was written by Moses in a book. 2 Chronicles 35:12.

Was placed in the side of the ark. Deuteronomy 31:24-26.

"Made nothing perfect." Hebrews 7:19.

Was nailed to the cross. Colossians 2:14.

Was abolished by Christ. Ephesians 2:15.

Was taken out of the way by Christ. Colossians 2:14.

Was instituted in consequence of sin. Leviticus 3-7.

haunted me long afterward. Obviously, somewhere along the line someone had failed. He, too, had discovered that the road of transgression of the principles of the Ten Commandments can be traveled only at one's own risk. He had found that "the way of transgressors is hard."

People in non-Christian countries tell us that the difference between the principles of our faith and the practice of our people is so great that they cannot see that we offer anything better than the heathenism they already have. What a sorry indictment of our lives! And yet we must confess that a glance at the lives of many nominal Protestants, Catholics, and Jews today would probably convince an onlooker that we have indeed discarded the Ten Commandments, no matter how much we might protest. Unfortunately, some unthinking churchmen only add to this conclusion by their thoughtless and groundless assertions that Christ destroyed the commandments when He died on Calvary's cross. These same confused individuals, however, later find it necessary to retrieve each commandment from the discard pile as they find its principles expressed anew by New Testament writers.

Just one verse of Scripture containing Christ's own words should forever convince us that Jesus did not destroy His law on Calvary's cross: "Think not that I am come to destroy the law. . . . Till heaven and earth pass, one jot or one tittle shall in no wise pass from the law, till all be fulfilled." Matthew 5:17, 18. Let us not make the mistake of misunderstanding the meaning of words as clear and plain as these.

Paul the apostle forever established the fact that the faith we Christians have in the finished work of Christ on Calvary does not in any way destroy or nullify the Ten Commandments. Here is how he puts it: "Do we then make void the law through faith? God forbid: yea, we establish the law." Romans 3:31. Those are strong words and impossible to misunderstand.

All the Bible writers are in perfect harmony on this subject. Here is how John expresses the same truth: "By this we know that we love the children of God, when we love God, and keep his commandments. For this is the love of God, that we keep his commandments." 1 John 5:2, 3. In the last book in the Bible, commandment keepers are referred to as God's saints: "Here is the patience of the saints: here are they that keep the commandments of God, and the faith of Jesus." Revelation 14:12.

James Russell Lowell was right when he said:

> "In vain we call old notions fudge,
>   And bend our conscience to our dealing;
> The Ten Commandments will not budge,
>   And stealing will continue stealing."

While by their lives some may seem to have discarded the Ten Commandments, it is important that we who have faith keep our thinking straight. If even some religious leaders among us rob the Ten Commandments of their validity and application to our day, we must not be surprised at the rising tide of lawlessness and delinquency which seems about to engulf us. We must then rightfully blame ourselves for destroying the dike that held back the flood!

Many, in attempting to discredit the Ten Commandments, have said that they belonged solely to ancient Israel and have no application in our day. Yet 2,500 years before the existence of the first Jew, it was wrong for Eve to covet the forbidden fruit; it was wrong for Cain to commit murder; it was wrong for the serpent to lie. The only part of the Bible written by God's own hand, these ten great rules have been binding upon all mankind from the very beginning, and are still binding today. What a protection the keeping of them would be to all of us!

Perhaps some of the arguments supporting the idea that the Ten Commandments were done away with by Christ stem from an honest misunderstanding of certain scriptures. Some are genuinely ignorant of the fact that the Ten Commandments, while separate and unique, are not the only set of laws in the Bible. In fact, in the Book of Exodus, the Ten Commandments (given in chapter 20) are immediately followed by a whole set of rather detailed laws. These had to do with the everyday practices of a faith which pointed forward to the coming of the Messiah. These laws had to do with the services of the sanctuary, where lambs were slain for sins, and certain prescribed ceremonies were carried out with their blood.

This law of ceremonies we commonly refer to as "the ceremonial law," even though that term as such does not appear in the Sacred Record. Other laws given by God applied specifically to the Jewish nation at the time of their encampment after their exodus from Egypt. These laws had to do with such things as sanitation in the camp of Israel and certain other matters which would have to be spelled out carefully in order for all to dwell together harmoniously. They, of course, were of temporary application, and could not be thought of as being universal in any sense.

The ceremonial law pointed forward with the blood of lambs and goats to "the Lamb of God, which taketh away the sin of the world." Obviously it would last only until the real Lamb appeared. When Christ died on the cross and said, "It is finished," the veil of the Temple was torn by the hand of God from top to bottom, thus signifying an end to the Temple worship and the law regulating it.

The writer to the Hebrews refers to the ceremonial law in this way: "Which stood only in meats and drinks, and divers washings, and carnal ordinances, imposed on them until the time of reformation." Hebrews 9:10. Of this law Paul, in writing to the Colossians, said, "Blotting out the handwriting of ordinances that was against us, which was contrary to us, and took it out of the way, nailing it to his cross." He then shows definitely that he was referring to the ceremonial law by the words which follow: "Let no man therefore judge you in meat, or in drink, or in respect of an holyday, or of the new moon, or of the sabbath days: which are a shadow of things to come; but the body is of Christ." Colossians 2:14, 16, 17.

It is the ceremonial law that contained references to meat and drink offerings, to the observance of the new moon, and to the celebration of the seven ceremonial sabbath days, such as the Passover, the Day of Atonement, etc. These things were all a shadow of things to come, pointing forward to the cross of Jesus Christ.

Christians no longer offer lambs for their sins, but they look back to the Lamb of Calvary who died for all of us upon a cruel tree. Neither do we celebrate the various feasts and holy days which also pointed forward to the cross. Rather, in baptism and the Lord's Supper, we celebrate reminders of His death, burial, and resurrection. In writing to the Ephesians Paul makes very clear what happened to the law of ordinances and ceremonies. He says, "Having abolished in his flesh the enmity, even the law of commandments contained in ordinances; for to make in himself of twain one new man, so making peace." Ephesians 2:15.

Religious leaders down through the years have understood the difference between these two laws, and the binding obligation upon all of us to keep the Ten Commandments. John Wesley, the Methodist leader, said, "This 'handwriting of ordinances' our Lord did blot out, take away, and nail to His cross. [Colossians 2:14.] But the moral law contained in the ten commandments, and enforced by the prophets, he did not take away. . . . The moral law stands on an entirely different foundation from the ceremonial or ritual law. . . . Every part of this law must remain in force upon all mankind, and in all ages."—*Sermons on Several Occasions,* Sermon XXV, "On the Sermon on the Mount" (2 vol. ed.), Vol. 1, pp. 221, 222.

John Calvin, Presbyterian, made this statement: "We must not imagine that the coming of Christ has freed us from the authority of the law; for it is the eternal rule of a devout and holy life, and must, therefore, be as unchangeable as the justice of God, which it embraced, is constant and uniform."—Comment on Matthew 5:17 and Luke 16:17, in *Commentary on a Harmony of the Gospels,* Vol. 1, p. 277.

The *Baptist Church Manual* contains this statement: "We believe that the moral law of God is the eternal and unchangeable rule of His moral government." Many other church creeds contain similar statements.

Someday every one of us is to be judged by how we have observed the Ten Commandments in our lives. Here is what we are told: "For whosoever shall keep the whole law, and yet offend in one point, he is guilty of all. For he that said, Do not commit adultery, said also, Do not kill. Now if thou commit no adultery, yet if thou kill, thou art become a transgressor of the law. So speak ye, and so do, as they that shall be judged by the law of liberty." James 2:10-12.

Are you living each day as an individual who will someday face the Ten Commandment law in the judgment? Let us not discard these great principles. We do so only at terrible risk and cost. Let us rather keep them gladly—all of them—remembering that Jesus our Saviour, who died for us on Calvary, wants us to do just that. Says the Apostle John, "For this is the love of God, that we keep his commandments: and his commandments are not grievous." 1 John 5:3.

Christ at the end of His life was able to say, "I have kept my Father's commandments, and abide in his love." John 15:10. By His grace and in His strength we may follow His example. If we slip and fall, we may ask His forgiveness and pardon and then take up again the privilege of a life of discipleship. To do this is my prayer and hope. Is it yours?

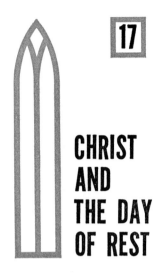

17

CHRIST
AND
THE DAY
OF REST

NOT LONG AGO I stood in what is left of old Capernaum on the shore of the Sea of Galilee. Capernaum is more than six hundred feet below sea level, and because of this low elevation the day was warm, even though it was wintertime.

Capernaum hardly exists today, for about all that is left are some ancient stone olive presses and the ruins of the town's only synagogue. Since Jesus referred to Capernaum as His own city, I suppose the synagogue might properly be called Jesus' own church. The roof is gone, and only stone ornaments carrying the chiseled-out forms of pomegranates, olives, and the star of David lie about the area.

Because this synagogue was rebuilt in the third century, not all of its ruins date back to Jesus' time; but as I walked among them, I felt that I was indeed treading ground made sacred by His presence nineteen hundred years ago. As I stood near the front of the edifice and looked at what must have been the place where the One bringing the message had stood, I could almost see Him standing there speaking some of His immortal words. This was the place where Jesus, when in Capernaum, spent a part of each Sabbath.

As I viewed this place made worthy of memory by His weekly presence, I could not help remembering that it was His method of enlightened Sabbathkeeping which had first brought Him the antipathy of those who later crucified Him. One day a man with a withered hand stood before Christ, asking to be healed. Christ knew that He was being observed by the scribes and Pharisees to see whether He would perform one of His miracles on the Sabbath. Despite this knowledge, He went right ahead.

Using the man as an object lesson, He asked those who thought evil against Him, "Is it lawful on the sabbath days to do good, or to do evil? to save life, or to destroy it?" Luke 6:9. After looking about upon the group, almost as a magistrate looking upon accused men, and failing to receive any reply from them, He turned His attention back to the needy man. He told him to stretch forth his hand; and when the hand was stretched forth, it was entirely normal. The result: "And they were filled with madness; and communed one with another what they might do to Jesus." Verse 11. Or as Mark expresses it, "The Pharisees went forth, and straightway took counsel with the Herodians against him, how they might destroy him." Mark 3:6. His doing good on the Sabbath brought "madness" to His enemies, who took counsel with *their* enemies, the Herodians, on how they might bring about His death.

This was not the only time Christ aroused the animosity of the religious leaders. Early in His ministry He had told an afflicted man to take up his bed and walk—another wonderful miracle of healing performed on the Sabbath. And the effect? "Therefore did the Jews persecute Jesus, and sought to slay him, because he had done these things on the sabbath day." John 5:16.

It is interesting to note that over the question of proper Sabbath observance the enemies of Christ first began to persecute Him and take counsel to kill Him. Sabbath observance has always been an issue used by those in the wrong to persecute their fellows. Not only was this attitude seen in Christ's day, but it also dogged America's Puritan pioneers who framed Sunday blue laws. It raises its ugly head even today in the rash of Sunday-closing laws being passed to force men to bend to the will of the majority.

The important thing for us to notice, however, was that the Pharisees were wrong in accusing Jesus of Sabbathbreaking. Though He was not keeping the Sabbath as they thought it should be kept, He was able to say of Himself toward the end of His life, "I have kept my Father's commandments." John 15:10. He did not in any way disobey the Father's expressed will as presented in the Decalogue. His sinless life has proved to all succeeding generations that men, with divine help, can keep the Ten Commandments.

His Sabbathkeeping was not acceptable to the Jewish leaders of the time because it was not in harmony with their petty laws by which they made Sabbath observance burdensome. Jesus, by His example and teachings, freed the Sabbath of these unscriptural restrictions and restored it to God's original intent—a day of communion with Heaven, a day of physical and spiritual refreshment, a day providing opportunities for doing good to mankind.

I thought of all this as I looked at Jesus' Sabbath home in Capernaum. I thought of it a few hours later as I journeyed the twenty miles up to old Nazareth, a city about fourteen hundred feet above sea level. There I visited a little ancient synagogue which probably stands on the place where the family worshiped when Jesus was a boy. It was thrilling to try to imagine Him in this environment so familiar to Him in the long ago.

But as far as buildings are concerned, perhaps of even greater importance today are the churches and chapels I have seen in the Americas, Europe, Africa, Asia—in fact, all around the earth—which are Sabbath homes for the followers of Jesus today. In these places His name is glorified, His power is felt, and His humble followers look expectantly toward the not-too-distant day when He will come again. As inspiring as it has been for me to walk about in the places where Jesus worshiped on the Sabbath when He was here upon this earth, I must admit that the little church where I as a boy worshiped on the Sabbath and the houses of worship where I subsequently have kept regular weekly appointments with my Saviour have done far more to change my life and have made more lasting impressions for good upon me.

It was Jesus' custom to attend the regular synagogue services on the Sabbath day. We are told in Luke 4:16, "As his custom was, he went into the synagogue on the sabbath day, and stood up for to read." The synagogue of Christ's time rejected Him and cast out His followers, who then were forced to meet in homes and upper rooms. I am convinced that inasmuch as we are told in Malachi 3:6, "I am the Lord, I change not," Jesus, if He were here today, would continue His custom of Sabbath worship. Without doubt He would seek out His followers to associate with them on the Sabbath day.

I shall never forget how Sabbathkeeping impressed me as a boy. My parents soon after their marriage came to sense the importance of a Christian's recognizing Jesus as his perfect example. They read the counsel of the Apostle Peter, who wrote long after the Saviour's ascension, "Christ also suffered for us, leaving us an example, that ye should follow his steps." 1 Peter 2:21. Interestingly enough, the Greek word translated "example" literally means an "underwriting," which in our terminology might be translated to mean "a carbon copy."

Jesus' life is the perfect pattern, and our lives are to be a carbon copy of His. As this great fundamental Christian truth dawned upon my father and mother, they were led to begin harmonizing their lives with that of Jesus, and as they did so, they started attending church on the Sabbath of Jesus—Saturday. After I came along, they taught me as a young boy what another of Christ's disciples had said in the later years of his life: "He that saith he abideth in him ought himself also so to walk, even as he walked." 1 John 2:6.

And so from earliest days I have known the joy of walking in the steps of Jesus in the matter of Sabbathkeeping as well as in other Christian ways. I was taught to love the Sabbath of Jesus just as I was taught to love everything else about my Saviour. And the Sabbath was a day to which I looked forward from week to week, for it was a day of special blessing and privilege.

You may have wondered if I did not think it strange that my family and the others in our church kept a day different from that observed by most of the Christian people in our community. Young people, and older ones too, ordinarily dislike being different; we all enjoy fitting into the accepted patterns. But as I look back, I realize that it did not disturb me to feel that I was different in a religious sense.

I had learned to love Jesus and had come to know that this was His Sabbath, and therefore it was mine also. As I grew older, I came to understand that in religious matters the majority has invariably been wrong—one therefore cannot in safety follow the crowd. I was glad to follow our perfect Example. The years which have come and gone have not changed that in any way. The Sabbath is still a delight to me, and I have had the privilege of passing along to my children my love for it as well as my love for the Saviour.

Perhaps the idea of a Christian keeping the seventh-day Sabbath, or Saturday, is a new idea to you. Even though now approximately two million people in the world are proud to consider themselves Sabbathkeeping Christians, still many have never heard the reasons why we believe as we do. Some have the idea that the Sabbath of the Old Testament is a different day from the Sabbath of the New Testament. They feel that when the word *Sabbath* is used in the Old Testament it refers to the day kept by the Jews, Saturday; but that when the word is used in the New Testament, it refers to the first day of the week, Sunday. Such is not the case.

Both the New Testament and the Old Testament refer to the same day when using the word *Sabbath*. This point is made very clear in Luke 23:54, 56 and 24:1. Speaking of the day on which Jesus was crucified, the record says, "And that day was the preparation, and the sabbath drew on." "And they returned, and prepared spices and ointments; and rested the sabbath day according to the commandment. Now upon the first day of the week, very early in the morning, they came unto the sepulchre, bringing the spices which they had prepared, and certain others with them."

These scriptures speak of the events commonly referred to as taking place on the weekend of Good Friday and Easter Sunday. Friday was the day on which Christ was crucified. It is referred to in the Bible as the preparation day—a day of preparation for the Sabbath. The next day, Saturday, is the "sabbath day according to the commandment." The day after the Sabbath is "the first day of the week"—the day on which Jesus was resurrected. Never in all the New Testament is the word *Sabbath* used to apply to Sunday. The Sabbath of the New Testament is the day just before the first day of the week. It is the day which was consistently observed by those associated with Jesus. It is the day which Jesus kept all His life and which He kept even in death, resting in the tomb on the Sabbath prior to His resurrection.

Some people mistakenly conclude that Christians should observe the first day of the week because on that day Christ rose from the dead. If Jesus had ever ordained such a plan, and if the Bible had ever made clear any such change, then there would be no question about Christian observance of Sunday. But the facts are that the New Testament is completely silent on any such theme. The Bible consistently, in both Old and New Testaments, speaks only of the Sabbath and speaks of it as being on the very same day.

One thing which interested me when I became old enough to really study this question thoroughly was to read every New Testament text referring to the first day of the week. There are not many. Let me list them here in order that you, too, may look them up and read them for yourself: Matthew 28:1; Luke 24:1; Mark 16:2, 9; John 20:1, 19; Acts 20:7; 1 Corinthians 16:2.

A reading of those texts does not give any indication whatsoever that God expected His people to be worshiping on the first day of the week, nor does it give any suggestion that the disciples actually *were* worshiping on the first day of the week, nor does it give any intimation that the disciples *expected* that *we* would worship on the first day of the week. A change of the Sabbath from Saturday to Sunday is absolutely not to be found within the covers of the Sacred Scriptures. The change can be found only in secular history, coming long years after the Bible had been completed.

One reference in the New Testament has puzzled some in that it refers to a meeting being held on the first day of the week. Some have thought that it indicates that the disciples were observing this day. The record is found in Acts 20:5-12. Note particularly verse 7: "And upon the first day of the week, when the disciples came together to break bread, Paul preached unto them, ready to depart on the morrow; and continued his speech until midnight."

Jewish reckoning began the day at sunset, as practically everyone knows, and by that system the dark part of the day of the week would be the night preceding Sunday, or our Saturday night. According to this reasoning, Paul's meeting at Troas began after sunset on Saturday night and continued through the night. The next day, Sunday, he walked on to Assos, using the day for travel and not for worship.

The eminent church historian Augustus Neander remarks in evaluating this passage as an evidence of early Christian Sunday-keeping, "The passage is not entirely convincing, because the impending departure of the apostle may have united the little Church in a brotherly parting meal, on occasion of which the apostle delivered his last address, although there was no particular celebration of a Sunday in the case."—*The History of the Christian Religion and Church,* Vol. 1, p. 337. There is indeed absolutely nothing to indicate that the disciples at this meeting were in any sense recognizing any sanctity in the first day of the week, nor were they in any sense observing this day in place of the Sabbath.

I have been told frequently that Sunday is "the Lord's day." The Bible does indeed use this expression, but it does not use it in either the New Testament or the Old to refer to the first day of the week. The Scriptures tell us in Luke 6:5: "And he [Jesus] said unto them, That the Son of man is Lord also of the sabbath." The consistency of the Scriptures on this point is vital. Never do we find Jesus referring to Himself as being Lord of any other day except the Sabbath. When John tells us in Revelation 1:10, "I was in the Spirit on the Lord's day," one can only conclude that he was referring to the Sabbath day—the same day of which Christ proclaimed Himself Lord.

Our heavenly Father, from the depths of His love for us, has given us ten rules for living—only ten—but they are so comprehensive that they include every avenue of life and indicate what path we must follow to secure the greatest amount of happiness. Disobedience to any one of His commandments really constitutes rejection of the Father who made us and the Saviour who redeemed us. Sabbathkeeping is not a question of legalism. It is a question of loving obedience of a child to his gracious and merciful Father and his kind and self-sacrificing Elder Brother.

I love the Sabbath of Jesus. I am happy to keep it in order that I may be in full harmony with the plan of God and of Christ for my life. I invite you to join me and millions of other Christians around the world in obedient dedication to the will of God. You will find as much joy in such service as I have found.

THE
HOLIEST
DAY

JUST BEFORE I was born, my parents were baptized and joined the church. They often told me when I was a small boy about the interest which developed in their hearts in a series of tent meetings conducted by an earnest worker for God in Bridgeport, Connecticut. As the result of their regular attendance at these meetings, they began to see religious matters in a new light and realized the necessity of making a complete dedication of their all to Christ. They never wavered for a moment in that dedication and never looked back with any longing upon what they had left.

When I was just three weeks old, they took me to the church and dedicated me to the Lord. I shall always believe that is why I am a minister today, for they ever kept before me the fact that they had given me to God and hoped I would find a place in His service. About twelve years later I was baptized in that same church, and more than twenty years later I was married in the same place. After I became a minister, it was my joy to preach there on a number of occasions.

As a child I learned to love the Sabbath of the Bible, a love which I have never outgrown. My parents kept the day strictly but never allowed it to become in any sense a burden to us children. Thus I do not remember the Sabbath as a day of restriction of my liberties, but rather a welcomed day of unusual opportunity. I have childhood memories of the Sabbath being a delight—a day for special activities together as a family that we did not have time for on other days, a day of worship together in a little church where we took a part in everything. And I do mean everything, for the church in which I grew up was exceedingly small—and really not very beautiful. Probably it would not seat even seventy-five people.

Instead of pews, we had rows of chairs attached together; and the chairs were stained rather than the windows. The organ was a little old-fashioned reed instrument which had to be pumped with the feet. Of course we had no choir. As I remember, we had practically none of the outward appurtenances which go to make a church and its services inspiring and lovely. But just the same, in the midst of our stark simplicity and lack of anything ostentatious, it was there that I gave my heart to the Lord Jesus Christ and felt the first stirrings of desire to go out in His vineyard and work for Him. I can never feel ashamed of roots like that.

Not long ago I received a letter from a man who had viewed my program on television. He wrote, "You seem to believe quite completely in the Bible. Why, then, do you not observe the seventh-day Sabbath of the Bible, which is the day we know as Saturday?" He was right, of course. Practically everyone knows that the Sabbath of the Bible is the day the Jews still observe—Saturday. And I have known it for a long time, too. It was therefore a pleasure for me to tell him that the seventh-day Sabbath is the very day my parents and my church taught me to love. It is the day I observe, for, you see, my parents were Seventh-day Adventists, and I am today a Seventh-day Adventist minister.

Because of my happy childhood memories and my joy in the Sabbath at present, I find it hard to understand completely the reluctance of some to keep God's Sabbath. I can never think of

Sabbath observance as any kind of unwanted burden imposed upon us by a difficult and exacting God who shows no understanding of today's problems. Rather, Sabbathkeeping is my response to a simple request made of me by the God who loves me and has always planned what is best for me and all the rest of His children. Surely it is not too much for Him to expect that I should obey Him in the faithful observance of His seventh-day Sabbath, no matter what anyone else thinks or does about it —is it?

Here is God's request exactly as He makes it in the fourth of the Ten Commandments: "Remember the sabbath day, to keep it holy. Six days shalt thou labour, and do all thy work: but the seventh day is the sabbath of the Lord thy God: in it thou shalt not do any work, thou, nor thy son, nor thy daughter, thy manservant, nor thy maidservant, nor thy cattle, nor thy stranger that is within thy gates: for in six days the Lord made heaven and earth, the sea, and all that in them is, and rested the seventh day: wherefore the Lord blessed the sabbath day, and hallowed it." Exodus 20:8-11. This command is specific and detailed, but it is not too much for Him to ask who has done so much for us and who still does so much for us each day of our lives.

But I do not keep the Sabbath out of a lifelong habit my parents instilled in me as a child. One does not continually swim against the stream out of habit; he has to have convictions. Since I have grown up, I have discovered that many otherwise good Christians seem to feel a real enmity against God's holy Sabbath. I have sat tensely in meetings where it was bitterly assailed by its enemies, and at other times I too have been bitterly assailed for defending it. Such experiences have forced me to search the Scriptures and my own soul diligently and exhaustively to discover what the Bible really teaches. And afterward I have had to make up my mind whether I really wanted to obey God regardless, or whether I wanted to follow the crowd. I observe the Sabbath today for reasons with which I am very well acquainted and which mean a great deal to me.

Have you ever realized that the Sabbath was given to man on the very first day of his life on earth? On the same day that he received life itself and the garden home in Eden, man also was introduced by God to the Sabbath. There can be no doubt that before sundown on that sixth day of creation week, God explained to Adam and Eve the place and purpose of the day which would follow. I believe that God and man rested together on that day and enjoyed spiritual refreshment and communion in their association.

That inspiring day was to serve as an example for all the Sabbaths to come. It must have been a wonderful experience for the newly created pair. I have an idea that they early learned to love the Sabbath. And I believe they loved and treasured it even more after their fall into sin, when they had to leave their beautiful garden home. The only lasting thing besides their marriage that they took with them from Eden was the Sabbath. It served as a constant link to, and reminder of, God and His loving care for them.

Here is how the Bible describes the making of the Sabbath on the seventh day of creation week: "Thus the heavens and the earth were finished, and all the host of them. And on the seventh day God ended his work which he had made; and he rested on the seventh day from all his work which he had made. And God blessed the seventh day, and sanctified it: because that in it he had rested from all his work which God created and made." Genesis 2:1-3.

Apparently it took three specific acts of God to make the seventh day different from the others, establishing it as the Sabbath. First of all, God *rested* on that day. Second, He *blessed* it; and third, He *sanctified* it. *To sanctify* means "to make sacred or holy; to set apart to a holy or religious use." God said something very significant when later He commanded men to "remember the sabbath day, to *keep* it holy." You see, God had made this day holy by His three special acts. We can *keep* holy only that which He has already *made* holy.

God has placed a special threefold blessing for each one of us in the Sabbath which has not been placed in any other day. I long ago became convinced that no matter how carefully an individual might attempt to observe any other day, he could not possibly "keep it holy," because it never was holy in the first place. But a Sabbathkeeper knows that great blessing accrues to his life every week as he keeps holy the day that God originally made holy.

I have heard it argued that Saturday is the Jewish Sabbath and Sunday the Christian Sabbath. Perhaps even you might have honestly thought this. But a little study on the subject will make you exclaim, "Where on earth did such an idea come from, anyway?" Certainly not from the Bible. The seventh-day Sabbath is not any more Jewish than was Adam himself. Moreover, marriage was given to Adam during the same creation week that the Sabbath was given to him, but I have noticed that no one ever tries to claim that marriage is for the Jews only!

Fifty-nine times in the New Testament the seventh-day Sabbath is mentioned, but never once is it spoken of as being changed or abolished. Eight times in the New Testament the first day of the week is mentioned, but never once is it called the Christian Sabbath, the Lord's day, or a day to be observed in honor of Christ's resurrection. Remember that each part of the New Testament was written between nineteen and sixty-three years after the resurrection; therefore any new customs intended for the early church would have had ample time to be mentioned.

The silence on any change forces us to conclude that sixty-three years after Christ arose from the dead His followers still knew nothing else but the same treasured Sabbath of the Old Testament. Paul kept the Sabbath, and though the Jews accused him of almost everything else, they never leveled a charge of Sabbathbreaking against him, because they could not.

But, of course, most important of all for Christians is the fact that our Example, Christ Jesus Himself, kept the Sabbath. "And he came to Nazareth, where he had been brought up: and, as his custom was, he went into the synagogue on the sabbath day, and stood up for to read." Luke 4:16. We are also told, "The Son of man is Lord even of the sabbath day." Matthew 12:8. The seventh-day Sabbath was Christ's Sabbath. It is the day of which He is Lord. Therefore, it is the Lord's day. It is the Christian Sabbath. No other day could possibly rightly claim these titles.

But why do I feel it important to observe the Sabbath? Of course, I could answer this quickly by saying that anything God requests should not be questioned by me, any more than I want my children to question a command I give them. On the other hand, ordinarily I am perfectly willing to explain to my children my reasons for expecting certain things of them. And God ordinarily is perfectly willing to explain the same things to us. Here is what He says: "Moreover also I gave them my sabbaths, to be a sign between me and them, that they might know that I am the Lord that sanctify them." Ezekiel 20:12. "And hallow my sabbaths; and they shall be a sign between me and you, that ye may know that I am the Lord your God." Verse 20.

The Sabbath, then, is a sign—a badge, if you please, which I may proudly wear as a sign or mark of allegiance to my heavenly Father. It represents in a special sense that He is the God whom I love and worship and who through Christ has made my sanctification possible. It is a special bond between God and me; and as I observe it, He blesses me. Through it I show Him that I love Him and remember His creative power, and thus I make Him supreme in my life. Reason enough!

After all the arguments are over, this is the conclusion of the writer to the Hebrews: "So then, there remains a sabbath rest for the people of God; for whoever enters God's rest also ceases from his labors as God did from his. Let us therefore strive to enter that rest, that no one fall by the same sort of disobedience." Hebrews 4:9-11, R.S.V.

Did you know that all the redeemed ones are going to keep the Sabbath in heaven? The Bible makes this clear. "For as the new heavens and the new earth, which I will make, shall remain before me, saith the Lord, so shall your seed and your name remain. And it shall come to pass, that from one new moon to another, and from one sabbath to another, shall all flesh come to worship before me, saith the Lord." Isaiah 66:22, 23. Since we are going to keep the Sabbath in heaven, don't you think it would be a good idea to start keeping it here? And remember, it is not difficult. It is not a burden. It is a tremendous joy and blessing. "For this is the love of God, that we keep his commandments. And his commandments are not burdensome." 1 John 5:3, R.S.V.

I love the Sabbath, God's Sabbath, the Christian Sabbath, the true Lord's day. I love the blessing which I receive each week in observing it. I love the peace it brings to my soul. I consider it a joy to follow my Lord and Master in Sabbathkeeping as well as in other matters when I remember how much He did for me and how much He loves me.

You too will love the Sabbath if you will keep it. Remember that you cannot *keep* holy any other day, for no other day *is* holy. Will you not enter, then, into the Sabbath rest with Christ, and finally enter into an abundant place in His kingdom? The Sabbath will come to mean as much to you as it does to me.

19

THE RIGHT TO BE RIGHT

WHY DO YOU persist in going to church on Saturday when all the rest of the world observes Sunday?" The question was honest and sincere and deserved an equally honest answer. The word *persist* seemed to accuse me—and the nearly two million other Christian Sabbathkeepers in the world—of stubbornness on this matter.

But in all fairness I do not believe myself ordinarily to be stubborn, and I patiently explained this in reply. Nor do I take any neurotic pleasure out of being different from the rest of the world or in seeming a bit "peculiar." In this one respect, at least, I fancy myself as being normal. I want to be considered a part of the group, accepted by others without reservation.

But I also like to envision myself as being willing to take a stand for what I feel is right, even if that might carry with it some liabilities. In fact, I do not really object to being different if I can feel absolutely certain in my own mind that the crowd is headed in the wrong direction. I would like to feel that I have principle enough to walk alone if need be, rather than to compromise with right so that I can be included with the majority. I cannot feel it in my heart even to be defensive about this outlook; actually, perhaps I might even be forgiven for a bit of just pride in it.

I explained to my questioner that in observing the Sabbath on the seventh day of the week I am obeying God's fourth commandment, which says, "Six days shalt thou labour, and do all thy work: but the seventh day is the sabbath of the Lord thy God: in it thou shalt not do any work." I continued that I observe the same Sabbath that Christ did—the Christian Sabbath. And since Jesus said, "The Son of man is Lord even of the sabbath day" (Matthew 12:8), in observing Saturday I know I am keeping the true Lord's day.

Further, I stated my convictions that the New Testament's complete and absolute silence on any change in the day of worship indicates that the apostles and early Christians were all Sabbathkeepers. Again and again this is implied in the Scriptures. To me it is all clear, plain, and consistent, with no need to attempt to "explain away" any seeming contradictions. Anyone who has ever studied the matter seriously, and particularly theologians of all faiths, should know that the Sabbath of the Bible is Saturday.

Then I returned the favor and asked the individual who questioned me, "Since the Bible is so clear that the seventh day is the Sabbath, why do you persist in observing the first day of the week, Sunday?" I have asked that question, in varying forms and under differing circumstances, of many people. And of course I have received many different answers. The usual reply is a good-natured shrug accompanied by an explanation that since almost everyone is doing it, it must be all right. But to me—and to all Christians who take the Bible as their sole rule of faith—such a reason could not be considered good enough.

When I was in Africa, I listened to the story of a native boy who had been attending a nondenominational mission school operated by Christians from the United States, Canada, and Great Britain. As a result of his study of the Bible, he was finally led to inquire of one of his teachers why this group observed

Sunday when the Bible specifically enjoined the observance of the seventh day.

Before the entire school this answer was given: "We do not know just when or how the change was made from Saturday to Sunday, nor do we know all the reasons behind it, but we feel that it must have been all right because a great deal of good has been accomplished by Christians through the years on Sunday." That answer was not good enough for the thoughtful native boy, and he became a Sabbathkeeper.

The convictions of a simple native boy securing an education are one thing, but what do the highly educated and noted church leaders say on this subject? As John Dowling, in his *History of Romanism,* says, "The Bible, and the Bible only, is the religion of Protestants! Nor is it of any account in the estimation of the genuine Protestant *how early* a doctrine originated, if it is not found in the Bible."

Dr. Liston Pope, dean of the Yale Divinity School, stated in a magazine article on this subject that in Christian history "the sanctions put on the Sabbath were transferred to the Lord's day, so that when this is read in a Christian Church, it means Sunday."—*Redbook* magazine, April, 1962. But there is no "Thus saith the Lord" for that statement, and to sincere and thoughtful Christians this must be the only test of any real merit.

Let us then squarely face the question. Where did Sunday observance really come from? How has it assumed such an important place in the Christian church? Many churchmen know, and they can tell us. Let us give them an opportunity to do so.

Edward T. Hiscox, D.D., was the author of *The Baptist Manual* and a respected and eminent theologian. Before a Baptist convention of ministers he made this statement:

"There was and is a commandment to keep holy the Sabbath day, but that Sabbath day was not Sunday. It will be said, however, and with some show of triumph, that the Sabbath was transferred from the seventh to the first day of the week, with all its duties, privileges, and sanctions. Earnestly desiring information on this subject, which I have studied for many years, I ask, Where can the record of such a transaction be found? Not in the New Testament, absolutely not. There is no Scriptural evidence of the change of the Sabbath institution from the seventh to the first day of the week.

"I wish to say that this Sabbath question, in this aspect of it, is the gravest and most perplexing question connected with Christian institutions which at present claims attention from Christian people."

Sir William Domville, a noted historian of the Church of England, asserted, "Centuries of the Christian era passed away before the Sunday was observed by the Christian church as a Sabbath. History does not furnish us with a single proof or indication that it was at any time so observed previous to the Sabbatical edict of Constantine in A.D. 321."—*The Sabbath: or an Examination of the Six Tests,* p. 291. This same historian also said, "Not any ecclesiastical writer of the first three centuries attributed the origin of Sunday observance either to Christ or to His apostles."—*Ibid.,* pp. 6, 7, supplement.

A few years ago Anglican Archbishop Philip Carrington gave an address in Toronto which was quoted in the Calgary *Albertan* (news item, October 28, 1949): "Carrington defiantly told a church meeting in this city of straight-laced Protestantism that tradition, not the Bible, had made Sunday the day of worship. He quoted the biblical commandment which said the seventh day should be one of rest, and then stated: 'That is Saturday.'

" 'Nowhere in the Bible is it laid down that worship should be done on Sunday,' the archbishop told a hushed, still audience.

"Local parsons read his comments today with set, determined looks. They refused comment."

Augustus Neander, a leading church historian of the Christian era, says, "The festival of Sunday, like all other festivals, was always only a human ordinance, and it was far from the intentions of the apostles to establish a divine command in this respect, far from them, and from the early apostolic church, to transfer the laws of the Sabbath to Sunday. Perhaps at the end of the second century a *false* application of this kind had begun to take place; for men appear by that time to have considered laboring on Sunday as a sin."—*The History of the Christian Religion and Church*, Henry John Rose's Translation, p. 186. (Italics supplied.)

The well-known Methodist clergyman Clovis G. Chappell has written, "The reason we observe the first day instead of the seventh is based on no positive command. One will search the Scriptures in vain for authority for changing from the seventh day to the first. The early Christians began to worship on the first day of the week because Jesus rose from the dead on that day. By and by, this day of worship was made also a day of rest, a legal holiday. This took place in the year 321.

"Our Christian Sabbath, therefore, is not a matter of positive command. It is a gift of the Church."—*Ten Rules for Living*, p. 61.

Here is another Methodist comment: "In the days of very long ago the people of the world began to give names to everything, and they turned the sounds of the lips into words, so that the lips could speak a thought. In those days the people worshipped the sun because many words were made to tell of many thoughts about many things. The people became Christians and were ruled by an emperor whose name was Constantine. This emperor made sun-day the Christian Sabbath, because of the blessing of light and heat which came from the sun. So our Sunday is a sun-day, isn't it?"—*Sunday School Advocate*, December 31, 1921.

Even Martin Luther commented on the subject: "They [the Catholics] allege the Sabbath changed into Sunday, the Lord's Day, contrary to the decalogue, as it appears, neither is there any example more boasted of than the changing of the Sabbath day. Great, say they, is the power and authority of the church, since it dispensed with one of the Ten Commandments."—*Augsburg Confession of Faith*, art. 28, par. 9.

Is it true that Catholicism does boastfully claim to have changed the day? Indeed so. The Catholic Bishop Eusebius, who presided in Caesarea in A.D. 330, writes, "All things whatever that it was duty to do on the Sabbath, these we have transferred to the Lord's Day."—*Cox's Sabbath Laws*, Vol. 1, p. 361.

Notice this almost derisive statement published in "The Question Box," *The Catholic Universe Bulletin*, 69 (August 14, 1942): "By what authority did the Church change the observance of the Sabbath from Saturday to Sunday?

"The Church changed the observance of the Sabbath to Sunday by right of the divine, infallible authority given to her by her Founder, Jesus Christ. The Protestant, claiming the Bible to be the only guide of faith, has no warrant for observing Sunday. In this matter the Seventh-day Adventist is the only consistent Protestant."

A host of other authorities could be quoted, but perhaps these will suffice. The plain facts are that Sunday is an institution of man, brought into being in direct contradiction to a divine edict of God as clearly expressed in the Ten Commandments. The church which made the change is proud of the fact and taunts those who claim the Bible as their only rule of faith and practice as not being consistent. The Catholic Church claims tradition and church rules as being of equal authority with the Bible. Though I have many Catholic friends for whom I have great respect and affection, I completely reject this claim, and I hope you and they do, too.

God was not taken by surprise when man attempted to change His law. Years ago He had foretold this very thing through the prophet Daniel. "He shall speak words against the Most High, and shall wear out the saints of the Most High, and shall think to change the times and the law." Daniel 7:25, R.S.V. And that is exactly what has been done. Men—fallible, finite, erring—have thought to tamper with the law of heaven, actually changing and altering the eternal law of the Almighty. In doing this they have placed their wisdom above His own. But despite their irreverent arrogance men could not really change His holy law. As the text points out, they have only *thought* to change it. But it will "stand fast for ever and ever."

In Paul's letter to the Romans occurs this thought-provoking statement: "Know ye not, that to whom ye yield yourselves servants to obey, his servants ye are; . . . whether of sin unto death, or of obedience unto righteousness?" Romans 6:16. The question is not so much which day you observe, although I am not one to minimize its importance. But rather the question is, Whom are you obeying? Whom are you serving? Do you take your stand with God, with Jesus Christ, with the patriarchs and prophets, and with the apostles? Or do you take your stand with the men who boast of their disobedience and with the mass of mankind which blindly follows after? I know with whom I stand. With Joshua of old I reaffirm, "As for me and my house, we will serve the Lord." Joshua 24:15. Will you do the same?

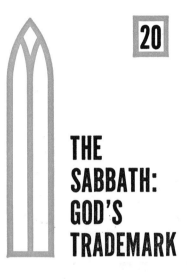

20

THE SABBATH: GOD'S TRADEMARK

EVERY SUNDAY afternoon in a certain city in Australia a sizable group of young people gather in the lounge room of the YMCA to watch the television program Faith for Today. Their readily apparent interest in what they see and hear has brought enough concern to one of the sincere officers of the organization to provoke him to write a courteous and restrained letter to me about it. It is not that he objects to the program, but he does feel distressed that it is presented by people who teach and observe the seventh-day Sabbath.

He enclosed a small red-covered pamphlet purporting to tell what was wrong with this doctrine. The author summed up his arguments in what he intended to be a short but stinging rebuke —"Sabbathkeepers are legalists." The writer of the letter requested my reaction.

Using the term "legalist" as if it were something repugnant is not new to me. But this time it forced me to do a little more thinking about it than usual. What is a legalist anyway?

Probably those making the charge of legalism mean to imply a dependence upon the keeping of the law for salvation rather than upon the sacrifice of Jesus Christ on Calvary. If such a charge is intended, it has no ground in fact, for a Christian Sabbathkeeper who is trusting in the Lord Jesus as his Saviour from sin is not trying to work his way to heaven. The Bible states, however, "Even so faith, if it hath not works, is dead, being alone. Yea, a man may say, Thou hast faith, and I have works: shew me thy faith without thy works, and I will shew thee my faith by my works." James 2:17, 18. Obviously, a workless faith is no faith at all. A genuine faith will naturally bear the fruit of good works.

The dictionary suggests that a legalist is one who advocates a strict and literal conformity to the moral code of the law, indicating that in this obedience there is something slavish, abnormal, and excessive. I readily grant that extremes in religious behavior are neither desirable nor attractive. But I am forced to face realistically the simple question, "Is it possible to be too law-abiding, conforming excessively to God's moral code? Have those who keep God's Sabbath 'gone off the deep end' in being overly literal in conformity to God's expressed will?" And if one argues that this is so, then are we to conclude that it is all right to be halfway in our obedience to the expressed will of God?

If there is some middle road in this matter of obedience, then to avoid being called legalists shall we keep all of the commandments half of the time, or shall we keep half of the commandments all of the time?

The plain fact is that probably such a charge would not be leveled if we would teach observance of nine of the commandments and the disregarding of the fourth. This leads us to ask in all candor, "Why does this antipathy exist? Why do some insist that we forget, or at least not interpret literally, the only commandment which God expressly prefaced with the word *remember*?" Without realizing it, of course, such individuals actually seek to obliterate something which God has always declared to be very important.

In seeking to do away with His Sabbath, people are doing away with that which God calls His "sign"; or to use a more modern expression, His "trademark." Years ago God expressed it this way: "Moreover also I gave them my sabbaths, to be a sign between me and them, that they might know that I am the Lord that sanctify them." Ezekiel 20:12. The Sabbath then occupied a distinctive place. As God's "sign" or trademark, its observance was to be recognized as a mark of loyalty and love for the God of heaven.

Once a year some countries of earth, notably the United States, celebrate a special day referred to as Mother's Day. Carnations are worn rather generally on that day—red for a living mother and white in memory of one who has passed away. The day serves as a time of reflection upon the blessings received from a beautiful and completely unselfish relationship—that of a mother to her child. When rightly observed, it serves to increase already existing bonds of affection, encourage the expression of genuine appreciation for a thoughtful mother, and increase family loyalty and devotion. This day of remembering the acts of kindness, the earnestness of purpose, the beautiful example, is never thought of by any right-thinking young person as dull, boring, "the most miserable day in the year." Rather, ideally it is a delightful day when hearts are warmed in remembering and communicating. But obviously for the day to mean anything, one must have known and appreciated the love of a mother.

Some of the reasons why mankind has felt the need for appointing a day for remembering the goodness of mothers prompted the appointment of a day in each week to remember the goodness of our heavenly Parent, the Creator of us all. The Sabbath was intended to be a uniting bond, knitting grateful man more closely with the One who made us in love and who has willed happiness for all. It is to be a day of *remembering* God's goodness and never-failing mercies, *expressing* our heartfelt gratitude, and *renewing* our happy relationship with our all-wise and benevolent Father.

Thus it becomes apparent that the Sabbath can be of no value whatsoever unless a man first feels something in his heart. He must feel devotion to God, appreciation for His blessings, and the rightness of His divine will expressed for us through the Ten Commandments. Just as Mother's Day must be more than a day for the wearing of carnations, so the Sabbath must be more than simply a day of refraining from labor. It has meaning only as it is representative of a happy and holy relationship.

Therefore if anyone is to properly observe the Sabbath, he must first of all have a living experience with God. The Sabbath is a sign, but it must be a sign of something. It is a sign that we know and love God, that Jesus Christ has been made the Lord of our lives, that we look back upon Calvary with recognition of our own sinfulness and the realization that upon the merciless cross Jesus paid the awful price for our redemption. Then in gratitude we happily wear the badge, the sign, the trademark, indicative of our experience with Him.

Fundamental and basic then to true Sabbathkeeping is the experience of conversion and the new birth. Without it the day can be little else than boring, and the hour spent in church going through the forms of the worship of God meaningless.

Apparently, when God created the Sabbath, He envisioned it as being the happiest and most anticipated day of the entire week. In fact, He even specifically stated His desire that we should look upon it as a "delight": "If thou turn away thy foot from the sabbath, from doing thy pleasure on my holy day; and call the sabbath a delight, the holy of the Lord, honourable; and shalt honour him, not doing thine own ways, nor finding thine own pleasure, nor speaking thine own words: then shalt thou delight thyself in the Lord." Isaiah 58:13, 14.

One thing is certain—the Sabbath can never be a very happy time if it is viewed negatively as a day of restrictions, inhibitions, repressions, and checks; if it is primarily a day of "don'ts." If the Sabbath is only a day in which we do nothing pleasant, and if the happiest thing about it is the going down of the sun to end it all, then it could never be refreshing and satisfying; it could never be eagerly anticipated and joyfully welcomed.

A number of years ago two brothers attended a series of evangelistic meetings and there learned what the Bible teaches, including the obligation of Sabbathkeeping. One brother decided that this was indeed God's message to him and took his stand, through baptism uniting with the church. The other brother rejected what he heard and lived his life as usual. The two lived in adjoining houses, and each Sabbath the new Sabbathkeeper sat on his front steps early in the morning and watched his brother leave for work. The brother would always call out, reminding him of how much money he was going to make that day—time and a half—and would ridicule him for not doing the same. At the end of the Sabbath, the brother who had worked would find and greet the brother who had not, reminding him again of how much better off he was financially as the result of having spent that day on the job.

Soon the new Sabbathkeeper was in a terribly jealous, confused, and frustrated state. His financial problems were so great that he needed to work at every possible opportunity, and yet his conscience was so tender that he felt he dare not desecrate God's Sabbath. Torn between the two, he was probably one of the unhappiest Sabbathkeepers that this world has ever seen. Soon he ceased attending church and sat about at home all day, talking constantly of the great loss that was his as the result of his Sabbathkeeping. The day had become to him a fearful chore, an oppressive obligation.

Happily for him, his attitude changed, or by this time he would be out of the church entirely. He finally came to recognize the wrongfulness of his point of view, and in time he came to see the Sabbath as the delightful, rewarding thing which God had intended it to be. He came to place full confidence in the God of the Sabbath who would never let him down if he faithfully followed Him. He has remained a faithful Christian in the years which have followed, and has even had the joy of seeing his brother ultimately take his stand for the Sabbath of the Lord as well.

The Sabbath is to be a delight. And so it can be. It is to be a day in which we joyfully "honour him." Anything which truly honors God and can be entered into with the objective of learning more of His character, works, ways, and will, is suitable for Sabbathkeeping. Anything which opens up avenues by which His love may be imparted to helpless and hopeless hearts about us is proper Sabbathkeeping.

The Sabbath can indeed be anticipated all through the week, because this day brings opportunity for soul-satisfying activities which are crowded out in the busy days of the work week. The converted child of God will want to associate with other Sabbathkeepers on this day because he needs the strength which such association will bring to him. He probably has confronted prejudice and scoffing for his faith during the week. He needs to associate with those who see things as he does to recharge his batteries and assure him again that despite the fact that at times he stands almost alone, he is doing right. And so the faithful Sabbathkeeper will surely be found in Sabbath School and church on that day, if at all possible.

But then during the rest of the day opportunities are provided to learn more of God through nature, through quiet walks in the fields and woods or by the streams. There are the opportunities to bring a little of God's love to those who know the meaning of suffering or the disappointments of loneliness and frustration. Sunshine bands, missionary visits, literature distribution, all have their place, and happily so, in making the day one filled with the rewarding activities which will make it a delight.

If the Sabbath is not a delight to you, if you may even be seeking a way to escape the obligation to keep it, look again at yourself and try to discover what is wrong. Ask first about your own Christian experience and see whether or not you know the meaning of conversion and the new birth. Remember that Christ wants to make you into a new creature so that old sins and desires and lusts will give way to the new life through Him. Face squarely the question that we so often ask in singing the old hymn: "Have you been to Jesus for the cleansing power? Are you washed in the blood of the Lamb? . . . Are your garments spotless, are they white as snow? Are you washed in the blood of the Lamb?" Remember that only souls who enjoy a close relationship with God can truly keep His Sabbath.

Then see whether or not you have been concentrating on the prohibitions of Sabbathkeeping rather than the opportunities. Push into the background of your mind the negatives, the things which we do *not* do on the Sabbath. Concentrate on the positives, the affirmatives, the opportunities which the Sabbath provides us each week. Then as you hallow God's Sabbaths, "they shall be a sign between me and you, that ye may know that I am the Lord your God." (Ezekiel 20:20.)

As converted believers we may be grateful for the privilege of understanding the days in which we live and of knowing of the nearness of the coming of our Lord. Of course, there are some things which, as Christians, we do not do, but there are many more things which we do. Our lives are rewarding and satisfying, not dull and unhappy. Instead of waking up in the morning with hangovers and "dark brown tastes," we can be inspired daily with the realization that God's mercies and blessings are "new every morning." Though the world will look upon us as being different—or at least we should be—we are happy with what we have through Jesus Christ. We proudly wear the badge, the trademark, the sign between us and God, and proclaim to the world our gratitude for a Saviour who gave Himself for us and a heavenly Father who loved us enough to give us His own Son.

21

THE PLEASURES OF NONCONFORMITY

WE WERE about thirty miles from Baghdad, traveling along a well-paved two-lane highway, when the driver said in a matter-of-fact tone, "We are now driving through the plain of Dura."

Startled out of my daydreaming, I looked at my physician friend, who was behind the wheel. "*The* plain of Dura?" I asked.

"*The* plain of Dura," he replied, and anticipating my request, pulled off on the shoulder of the road.

I looked about me at the flat country, broken only by an occasional cone-shaped brickkiln. The words "plain of Dura" conjured before me a scene that had taken place thousands of years before, during the reign of King Nebuchadnezzar and the lifetime of Daniel the prophet. Here three staunch and fearless Hebrews were cast into a burning fiery furnace because of their refusal to bow before a great metal image.

The sky was heavily clouded, and the wind, forerunner of a driving rainstorm, blew in our faces as we stood thoughtfully on the almost deserted plain. Beside us I could imagine the three Hebrews standing. Convinced that they should worship only God, they had refused to bow before a great image erected by

King Nebuchadnezzar of Babylon. Their high courage in the face of threatened death, their loyalty to minority religious concepts in spite of overwhelming pressures from the majority, their tenacity despite universal capitulation to an unjust demand, have inspired succeeding generations similarly called upon to compromise their faith.

Do you remember the story? Nebuchadnezzar, some years before Decision Day on the plain, had dreamed about a great metal image with head of gold, breast and arms of silver, belly and thighs of brass, legs of iron, and feet partly iron and partly clay. Daniel, a prophet of God, had correctly interpreted this inspired dream as indicating the rise and fall of the world empires of Babylon, Medo-Persia, Greece, and Rome, followed by Rome's disintegration into subdivisions. You may read the entire story in Daniel 2 in the Bible. Nebuchadnezzar had been gratified at the interpretation, "Thou art this head of gold," but he had not liked the idea that his kingdom would someday be superseded by another. Therefore, he was immensely pleased when years later some of his princes suggested the building of a similar image on the plain of Dura to be made *entirely* of gold. If he had anything to do with it, Babylon would last forever.

In due time the image was constructed. Towering as high as a ten-story building, it must have commanded for many miles the attention of travelers approaching the capital city of Babylon. On the day the image was to be dedicated, leaders from all over the realm were brought in to participate. Among them were three Hebrews.

But then the blow struck! The assembled multitudes were told that when they heard the ancient equivalent of our Marine Band strike up their equivalent of our national anthem, everyone was to bow down in worship before the image! Any person refusing to do so would be burned alive. Before that time nothing had been said about worship of the image. Without doubt, everyone had considered it to be only a new national symbol and one's presence at its dedication desirable as a demonstration of patriotism. Now duty to God and duty to state clashed, producing turmoil in the hearts of honest men who served both.

What thoughts must have raced through the minds of the three Hebrews! Escape was impossible; any attempt to leave the vast throng would be immediately noticed. Should they make their way to the king to personally object and to explain the reason why they could not conform? There was no time for that. They could not be unaware of the reaction of the people about them, who would label them "traitor," "yellow-bellied," or even the "commies" of their day. Unimpassioned consideration of their religious scruples could not be expected when the issues had become so muddied and the mob-thinking so muddled.

Hopeless was the position of these loyal subjects of the king. Despite their desire to support country and government in every way possible, they recognized that their primary loyalty to the supreme sovereignty of God left them no alternative but reluctant disobedience. So complete was their commitment to God that they chose the promised horrible death rather than perform an act indicating rejection of Jehovah.

Enlightened governments never make such a choice necessary. But Babylon was not enlightened. Church and state were united in the person of the king. And now the consequences of that union were to be demonstrated.

As everyone else bowed, the three Hebrews remained stiffly erect. I have never been able to convince myself that they were the only worshipers of God in that vast crowd. Because Israel at that time was a captive nation in Babylon, I believe it highly improbable that such a large and well-publicized assemblage contained only three Israelites. But if other Hebrews were present, one thing becomes self-evident—*they bowed*. When the pressure became too great, they capitulated. Only three had the courage of their convictions.

What would a Hebrew who bowed say to the three who would not? I can imagine one whispering, "Get down, you fools! You can believe in your heart whatever you want, but don't take a chance on your lives. What good will you be to anyone as martyrs? Get down with the rest of us!" But the daring men of conviction remained stoically unmoved.

Years later similar unbending religious convictions forced an intrepid band of Pilgrims to risk their lives on the high seas of the Atlantic in a tiny ship, seeking a land where they too could worship God according to conscience. On numerous occasions I have looked down on Plymouth Rock and tried to imagine them setting foot on the new shore and subsequently founding a colony that provided the religious freedom which meant more to them than life. Every American who has not forgotten his country's heritage can identify with these three Hebrew worthies.

What must it have been like to have the stern eyes of an incredulous nation upon them? Sense the anger of the king. The eyes of the nation were upon him, too. His prestige was at stake, as was the security of the nation. Was not the defiance of the Hebrews part of a plot to undermine the confidence of the people in Babylon's future? Due process of law imposed no great barrier to the king's wrath. Punishment for misdeeds could be both arbitrary and immediate.

The king speaks. And the measure of his forbearance can be found in this—he gave the three men another chance. The band would play again. If at the sound of the music they would fall down and worship the image, all would be well.

"But if ye worship not," said the angry king, "ye shall be cast the same hour into the midst of a burning fiery furnace; and who," he added with a sneer, "is that God that shall deliver you out of my hands?"

But their minds were made up. They needed no second chance. Neither national disapproval nor kingly scorn could turn these men from their convictions. The king was a man of his word; they were consigned to the fiery furnace. This was no ordinary punishment. Few references in history are made to this means of execution. The king undoubtedly used something immediately available—a brickkiln. Excavations show that the ancient brickkilns were similar in construction to the modern ones found in that area in great numbers.

As we stood on the plain of Dura that day, thinking of past events, my friend suggested that I dip my finger in a nearby puddle of water and tell him what it smelled like.

"Oil," I replied.

"You find it all over this country," he said. "It was the obvious fuel for firing bricks."

Anciently the fuel, a mixture of crude oil and chaff producing an intense heat, was introduced through an opening on one side of the round structure. This opening also provided a view of the inside.

With the first drops of the approaching rain splashing on my face, I recalled the inspiring conclusion of the ancient story. As the multitude watched breathlessly, the three men were hurled into a nearby brickkiln heated far beyond its ordinary maximum. Instant death followed—not for the victims but rather for the executioners.

If the king, seated nearby observing the proceedings, was unnerved by this, soon thereafter he was startled beyond measure. Jumping to his feet in astonishment, he cried to those around him, "Did not we cast three men bound into the midst of the fire? They answered and said unto the king, True, O king. He answered and said, Lo, I see four men loose, walking in the midst of the fire, and they have no hurt; and the form of the fourth is like the Son of God." Daniel 3:24, 25.

Have you ever wondered how the king knew what the Son of God looked like? One answer presents itself: These Hebrews had not been quiet regarding their beliefs. They had spoken of their conviction that someday soon the Messiah would appear. When the king saw the glorious form of the fourth man in the fiery furnace, perhaps he concluded that the moment of the arrival of the Messiah had come. In a vital moment of clarity he saw that the religious convictions of these men had been right after all, and he recognized the wrongfulness of his own action. Calling into the fiery furnace, he asked the men who were there to come out. The three who had been cast in did so, and the fourth, needed no longer, disappeared.

When the three stood again before the king, he found that the fire had not harmed them. Their hair had not been singed, their clothing was undamaged, and they did not have upon them even the smell of fire. By a miracle God had preserved those who had honored Him.

The monarch concluded his dedication services for the image by speaking a blessing for the God of heaven who had "delivered his servants that trusted in him, and have changed the king's word, and yielded their bodies, that they might not serve nor worship any god, except their own God." (Daniel 3:28.) The king then made a decree that no one should ever speak anything against the God of these three men, threatening that any who did would be cut in pieces and their houses destroyed, because, he affirmed, "there is no other God that can deliver after this sort." (Verse 29.)

In the king's enthusiasm he went too far, for it is as wrong to make religious laws compelling people to recognize or serve the true God as it is to make laws compelling them to recognize or serve any other. Worship is a personal and voluntary matter between each man and his God. Religious laws have no legitimate place in an enlightened society.

To escape the rain, which by now had begun in earnest, we dashed to the protection of our waiting car. Soon we were moving again, more slowly now, on the rain-splashed, glistening pavement.

As we drove, I knew that not far from the ancient plain unfair laws were being enforced, curtailing the religious freedoms of civilian populations. Government-placed padlocks were hanging ominously from the front doors of some churches. A Bible correspondence school, doing nothing worse than acquainting men and women with the Word of God, had been closed and its records seized. The shadow of government confiscation hung over the very church-built hospital of which my physician friend was the medical director. Only a few days later that shadow fell, and he was forced to leave the country.

Even in twentieth-century America images are being erected, minority opinions are increasingly being equated with threats to national security, and the rumble of the mob can be heard: "Get down! On your knees!"

"Mass opinion has acquired mounting power in this century," Walter Lippmann observes in his book *The Public Philosophy*. "It has shown itself to be a dangerous master of decisions when the stakes are life and death."—Quoted in *U.S. News and World Report*, April 22, 1955.

Recently, as a member of a minority Christian group, I stood in court accused of "Sabbathbreaking." I had worshiped on the seventh-day Sabbath, as the law of God commands. But the state had its image and its law to force conformity. Not, of course, a fiery furnace for dissenters. Only a fine. But perhaps here, too, someday the band will play and the crowd will bow. And again men will need to remember three Hebrews—and a fourth like the Son of God—and courage on the plain of Dura.

WHEN DEVILS WORK MIRACLES

THE SCRIPTURES foretell that in the last days of earth's history the devil will work in a strong way against the church. Part of that work will be conducted through the miracle-working power of spiritism—the spirits of devils working miracles in the sight of men. And men will be deceived into believing falsehoods and accepting ideas contrary to those expressed in the Word of God.

By these miracles the devil will make it seem as if the Bible's teachings are erroneous. As the result, God's people will have to stand alone in their unpopular beliefs, having only the certainty that these are sustained by the Word of God, in which they have utmost confidence.

Three texts of Scripture indicate these facts: "And the dragon was wroth with the woman, and went to make war with the remnant of her seed, which keep the commandments of God, and have the testimony of Jesus Christ." Revelation 12:17. "And he doeth great wonders, so that he maketh fire come down from heaven on the earth in the sight of men." Revelation 13:13. "For they are the spirits of devils, working miracles." Revelation 16:14.

Without doubt, not all will recognize the insidious nature of the devil's warfare. We may expect spiritism to make important inroads into the church as a whole, thus preparing the way for final deceptions. While as yet fire has not descended, already it is possible to see the beginnings of the fulfillment of these prophecies.

In the March 12, 1958, issue of *The Christian Century,* in some ways the foremost Protestant journal published today, an article appeared which startled me. It tells of the growing interest in "extra-sensory perception and the psychic." These are modern expressions used frequently to refer to spiritism.

The article describes the formation in 1956 of an organization called the Spiritual Frontiers Fellowship, made up principally of orthodox Protestants who have banded together to delve into "psychical research," and tells of the formation in England of a similar group, called the Churches' Fellowship for Psychical Study. One of the aims of this group is to afford opportunities where church members can "consult tested, trusted Christian 'sensitives' dedicated to God for this purpose." The words *seer* and *sensitive* refer to spiritistic mediums.

The article comes to grips with some of the problems which Protestant churches might have to face as their members come to depend too much on the church-sponsored mediums for daily guidance. Not solved is the problem of how to encourage people to make decisions and avoid turning over their lives entirely to those in whom they would come to have confidence.

Imagine a prominent religious journal carrying a proposal as monstrous as this—spiritistic mediums set up in offices in the church, where church members can come to consult them about their lives! The article asserts that in both England and America these organizations already have several thousand members, a large percentage of whom are Protestant clergymen!

One of the leaders of this new group in America is Arthur Ford. In a recent autobiography he has told the story of how he started his professional life as a Protestant minister but soon became aware that he possessed unusual powers as a medium. Ultimately he resigned his pulpit and devoted his life to giving demonstrations of the occult on the lecture platform. At present he travels about, speaking to ministerial groups everywhere and encouraging Protestant ministers to become a part of the Spiritual Frontiers Fellowship. He asserts that through spiritism and its miraculous manifestations Protestantism will regain the divine power which once it had. His teachings are being widely accepted, and the influence of the Spiritual Frontiers Fellowship is growing. Through this organization Protestantism seems indeed to be reaching across the gulf to clasp the hand of spiritism.

Not long ago I visited an art gallery and museum in an Indiana town where a spiritistic camp is operated. I did not realize until I was inside that the art gallery was connected with the camp. One of the most interesting parts of the visit was my conversation with the curator, whom I discovered to be a dedicated spiritist. During his lifetime he asserted he had seen a great change in the climate in which spiritism works.

Forty years ago, when he united with a spiritist church, he stated that Protestant churches would have nothing to do with his church or its teachings, feeling that spiritism was of the devil. "But now," he declared, "that is all different. Thousands of Protestant ministers preach our doctrines from their pulpits. Men who are well known everywhere and who have never identified themselves outwardly with spiritism are publicly preaching just exactly what we believe. They need not identify with us in church membership. It is all right with us for them to stay where they are and continue their good work."

At my request he willingly named a number of well-known Protestant ministers whom he considered to be believers in spiritism's teachings. In attempting to prove his assertion, the curator referred to an October, 1957, *Reader's Digest* article which had a direct quote from a book by Dr. Norman Vincent Peale.

Dr. Peale writes: "The day I received the news that my

mother had died I went to my church in New York City and sat in the pulpit. I wanted to feel Mother's presence; she had always told me, 'Whenever you are in that pulpit, I will be with you.'

"Then I went into my study. On the table was an old, tattered Bible that I always take with me wherever I go. In an instinctive desire for comfort that day, I placed my hand on it. As I stood looking out toward Fifth Avenue, I suddenly and distinctly felt two cupped hands, soft as eider down, resting very gently on my head. It was a feeling of inexpressible joy. . . .

"From that moment on I have never doubted my mother's spiritual aliveness. I *know* that she lives and that she will live forever." (Taken from *Stay Alive All Your Life.*)

The museum curator related another story from one of Dr. Peale's earlier books, telling of his visit to his mother's grave in a little cemetery in Ohio: "Suddenly he heard a voice, her voice, speak to him. He quoted her as saying, 'Why seek ye the living among the dead?' And from that moment on, Dr. Peale has not thought of his mother as being in that cemetery at all but rather as being right with him at all times."

From personal observation and contact I believe Dr. Peale to be a dedicated man. However, I fully recognize that the most sincere men may be unaware of the workings of the master deceiver and may, therefore, play right into his hands. In spiritism Satan works upon man's tenderest emotions to bring about his deceptions. The current, but unscriptural, belief that man is by nature immortal originated with the Greek philosopher Plato. But in its earliest form this philosophy was expressed by the devil to Eve in the Garden of Eden when he contradicted God's statement and affirmed, "Ye shall not surely die: . . . ye shall be as gods." Genesis 3:4, 5. But those who are Christ's will have immortality conferred upon them at our Lord's second coming, and the Scriptures teach that now only God has immortality. (1 Timothy 6:15, 16.)

The curator then referred to another prominent Protestant

minister, Dr. Marcus Bach, whom he stated had accepted and was now propagating the beliefs of spiritism. Dr. Bach originally started as a Methodist minister and is now a teacher at the University of Iowa. His writings are widely quoted. He has written a book entitled *The Will to Believe*. Dr. Bach in his book encourages Protestants—and everyone else—to look more closely at what he describes as three worlds: the world within us, the world around us, and the world beyond us, which is his way of referring to the world to which he believes the dead have gone.

In this book Dr. Bach tells how he became convinced that spiritism's claims are justified. For some time he had wondered about the possibility of communicating with the dead. In his pursuit of information, he had attended many spiritistic séances —a practice, incidentally, which I feel to be extremely dangerous. His search led him finally to Chesterfield, Indiana, and to a séance conducted by a medium who had promised to bring forth spirits in visible form so that those present could see them as well as talk with them, a process referred to as "materialization."

Dr. Bach states that the basement room in which the séance was conducted had been darkened by covering the windows with venetian blinds and black velvet curtains. The only light came from a spotlight on the wall which had been carefully covered with a piece of red gelatin paper. The medium entered the room and seated herself in a "cabinet," which was made out of black velvet curtains hung from the ceiling. Her assistant stood outside, and the group of seven witnesses waited for something to happen. The assistant told the group that the medium was now going into a trance. They were requested to be in a "reverent" state of mind.

It was suggested that to use the time, they join in singing. Seated in a semicircle, the group sang "I Heard the Voice of Jesus Say." After only one stanza, they heard the high-pitched, childlike voice of a spirit, who identified herself as "Twilight." She giggled and spoke to them in what Dr. Bach considered silly and childish babblings.

Then a light flickered near the floor, giving a luminous glow which came suddenly but soon began to fade away. Then the light loomed again, but this time became "bright and shimmering." And out of its vortex a form began to appear. Dr. Bach described something like shoulders and then a face appearing "as the luminescent stuff swirled into bodily form. Then a voice called one of the women in our circle by her first name. The woman got up, took a few steps, and said to the materialized form, 'Yes, Mother?'"

The spirit asked in a low whisper, "How are you?"

The woman replied, "I'm fine. Why didn't you bring Father with you?"

Immediately another form appeared behind the first, and a man's voice said, "She did."

Then a third form, that of a young boy, appeared, and this one referred to the lady in the circle as his mother. The child whispered, "Mother, do you remember the walks we used to take? . . . Let's take one now." He stepped over to her, took her by the arm, and they began to walk about the room, coming so close to Dr. Bach that he found it necessary to draw back his feet.

After an hour it seemed as if most of those in the circle, except Dr. Bach, had talked with some spirit which claimed to be a loved one. "Then the swirling ectoplasmic stuff rose from the floor to take on the form of a girl. As she grew, she spoke in a whisper: 'Marc, dear. . . . Marc, dear. . . . Marc, dear.'" That is Dr. Bach's first name—Marcus. He stood and stepped closer to the vaporlike spirit, asking, "Who are you?" She replied, "Don't you know me? Paula." His sister Paula had died twenty years before, at the age of twenty-three. He could hardly remember what she looked like, but the apparition standing before him seemed to have her appearance. They talked together, and she brought him "greetings" from other departed loved ones. This made him more certain that it was really she.

Yet he was still not positive that she really was what she claimed to be. So he asked her what he considered to be a test question: "Paula, do you remember the catechism we kids learned at home? . . . What is the first question in that catechism?" She replied accurately, " 'What is your chief comfort in life and in death?' " When she stopped, he asked her to continue, and she did so without difficulty.

She asked if he had questions, and he responded that he had many. He asked her a few, including whether or not she had ever seen Jesus Christ. She answered, "No one has seen Jesus. He is in the philosophers' heaven."

Finally her whispering grew fainter, and she announced that she would have to leave. Since Dr. Bach wanted to get a little closer look at her, he asked if she would be willing to put her arms around him. She replied affirmatively and offered to give him a kiss as well. She stepped toward him, and her face was well illuminated by the red light from over his shoulder. He felt something like arms go around his neck, felt the brush of a kiss on his forehead, and then she dematerialized down through the floor. When the séance ended, Dr. Bach walked out of the room a firm believer in the ability of living people today to contact and talk with the spirits of their departed dead.

Dr. Bach in his book has mentioned the names of others who, he states, believe as he does. He refers to Dr. Joseph R. Sizoo and quotes a statement which this eminent churchman made in writing an introduction to Albert Payson Terhune's *Across the Line*. The statement says, "The human heart has always rebelled against the silence of death. . . . Here is the record of one who makes the great affirmation that it [communication] is not only possible, but that it has been experienced. This is not the first voice that has protested against the silence of death and cried out exultantly, 'I have heard and I have seen.' God has given to the spiritually sensitive to lift the curtain for us and let in the light."

Dr. Bach himself states, "In this religiously intensified age man feels both courageous and free to find 'truth' wherever truth is found. You will not frighten him from the quest about life after death with isolated Scripture texts, not even with Paul's admonition to the Romans, 'Stay away from those who have familiar spirits.' "—*The Will to Believe*, p. 154.

Dr. Bach quotes E. Katherine Bates, who gives instruction for contacting the departed dead of one's own family. The instruction appears to be a form of self-hypnosis which involves close and careful concentration on the individual whom one wishes to contact and a calling of the name of the departed one, speaking to him as if he were close by. Then this statement appears: "If you persevere, some realization of the presence of the beloved one will come to you, so undeniable and so convincing to your own consciousness that a whole college of philosophers or scientists will not be able to persuade you that the one you loved and lost was not in close touch with you." (From *Do the Dead Depart?*)

How contrary all this is to the clear and plain teachings of the Word of God! "As the cloud is consumed and vanisheth away: so he that goeth down to the grave shall come up no more. He shall return no more to his house, neither shall his place know him any more." Job 7:9, 10. According to the Bible, it is impossible for the dead to come back to deliver messages to the living, as spiritism claims, for they peacefully sleep, awaiting the resurrection.

In the Old Testament God strongly condemned mediums and their fraudulent messages coming neither from the dead nor from God. Here is His counsel: "Do not turn to mediums or wizards; do not seek them out, to be defiled by them: I am the Lord your God." Leviticus 19:31, R.S.V. "There shall not be found among you . . . any one who practices divination, . . . or a medium, or a wizard, or a necromancer. For whoever does these things is an abomination to the Lord." Deuteronomy 18:10-12, R.S.V. Under the theocracy of ancient Israel, God even commanded, "A man or a woman who is a medium or a wizard shall be put to death." Leviticus 20:27, R.S.V.

He gives this further counsel: "And when they say to you,

'Consult the mediums and the wizards who chirp and mutter,' should not a people consult their God? Should they consult the dead on behalf of the living?" Isaiah 8:19, R.S.V. God's people are expressly forbidden to seek and consult with mediums.

God recognized that just before Christ's coming there would be a great upsurge of spiritistic manifestations. "Now the Spirit speaketh expressly, that in the latter times some shall depart from the faith, giving heed to seducing spirits, and doctrines of devils." 1 Timothy 4:1. It may astonish some to learn that those who seek out spirits have departed from the faith and are following doctrines of devils. Strong language indeed. The devil himself masquerading as "an angel of light" is the power behind the pretentions of spiritism. No wonder God's warnings are so strongly stated!

x The world has yet to see the extent to which Satan will go to draw multitudes away from true faith. "As the crowning act in the great drama of deception, Satan himself will personate Christ. The church has long professed to look to the Saviour's advent as the consummation of her hopes. Now the great deceiver will make it appear that Christ has come. In different parts of the earth, Satan will manifest himself among men as a majestic being of dazzling brightness, resembling the description of the Son of God given by John in the Revelation. The glory that surrounds him is unsurpassed by anything that mortal eyes have yet beheld. The shout of triumph rings out upon the air, 'Christ has come! Christ has come!' The people prostrate themselves in adoration before him, while he lifts up his hands, and pronounces a blessing upon them, as Christ blessed His disciples when He was upon the earth. His voice is soft and subdued, yet full of melody. In gentle, compassionate tones he presents some of the same gracious, heavenly truths which the Saviour uttered. . . .

"But the people of God will not be misled. The teachings of this false christ are not in accordance with the Scriptures. . . .

"And, furthermore, Satan is not permitted to counterfeit the manner of Christ's advent. The Saviour has warned His people against deception upon this point, and has clearly foretold the manner of His second coming. 'There shall arise false christs, and false prophets, and shall show great signs and wonders; insomuch that, if it were possible, they shall deceive the very elect. . . . Wherefore if they shall say unto you, Behold, He is in the desert; go not forth: behold, He is in the secret chambers; believe it not. For as the lightning cometh out of the east, and shineth even unto the west, so shall also the coming of the Son of man be.' This coming, there is no possibility of counterfeiting. It will be universally known—witnessed by the whole world."—Ellen G. White, *The Great Controversy*, pp. 624, 625.

In fact, the Bible goes even further: "For the living know that they shall die: but the dead know not any thing, neither have they any more a reward; for the memory of them is forgotten. Also their love, and their hatred, and their envy, is now perished; neither have they any more a portion for ever in any thing that is done under the sun." Ecclesiastes 9:5, 6. Only in the resurrection morning will God's children live again. (1 Thessalonians 4:16, 17.)

H. E. Boyer, while pastoring a church in Anderson, Indiana, adjacent to suburban Chesterfield, told me an interesting story regarding the construction of his lovely new church building. One of the last purchases made was that of the wooden front doors. Pastor Boyer made this purchase from the same concern from which he had bought a number of other parts of the structure. After the transaction was completed, the gentleman who ran the establishment told him, "This will probably be the last purchase you will be able to make from me, because I am selling out."

In answer to the pastor's questions, he explained that he was going to spend his time in the manufacture and sale of an invention of his called "ultravision." He described it as being something like a television set but lacking the tubes and other paraphernalia upon which an ordinary television set depends. On the picture portion of an ultravision set images appeared, not from a television studio, but rather, of the departed dead, who could be seen and heard. These images could actually carry on a conversation with the people in the room. He said that on numerous occasions recently he had seen and talked with his departed mother and had tape recordings of their visits together.

Finally, this gentleman claimed to have seen Jesus Christ twice on his ultravision set! But the "Christ" on the ultravision laughed off a question about the Bible and said the instructions found there were not essential.

Do you suppose that Christ today would give instruction contrary to that which is contained in His Word? The Bible has said, "To the law and to the testimony: if they speak not according to this word, it is because there is no light in them." Isaiah 8:20.

Our only safeguard against the devil's last-day deceptions is in being so firmly established in the teachings of the Word of God that we will recognize the counterfeit, no matter how much like the genuine it may appear. Such knowledge can come only through renewed reverence for the Bible and earnest daily study of its teachings. In this way we will be fortified.

23

FAITH'S PERFECT POWER

ONE HALLOWEEN night when I was thirteen, I joined three of my school chums to hobnob with the goblins of the season. Under cover of darkness we engaged in the usual pranks, which we hoped would somehow prove to be truly devastating to the hapless and unsuspecting victims.

We did not know anything about "trick or treat" in my day. It was all trick for us, the tricks confining themselves primarily to the ringing of doorbells and the subsequent running as if for dear life down the street. At times, however, we engaged in what we considered the height of perverse wickedness and inserted a pin in the doorbell, causing it to continue ringing steadily until the pin was discovered and removed by the occupants of the house.

As the hour drew near when our parents expected us to be in for the night, we turned reluctant steps homeward through the city's streets. Suddenly one of the boys (he is a practicing physician today) pointed to a loaded and temporarily unattended beer truck parked across the street and ran quickly toward it. Not knowing what trick he had in mind but more than willing to find out, we joined him.

172

When he arrived at the rear of the open truck, he reached up into it, saying, "Grab a bottle and run." While the other three reached and grabbed, I hesitated. They waited for a moment to give me encouragement, but I still did not budge. Then, realizing the danger of further delay, they rushed off, and I followed empty handed close at their heels.

A block or two later, when they had determined that we had not been followed, they stopped in a vacant lot to consider the situation. Despite their irritation at my having been "chicken," they generously offered to share the spoils with me. Since only one of the group had ever tasted an alcoholic beverage before, it was evident that each looked upon this as a rare opportunity for widening horizons. They eagerly worked the caps off the bottles, thoroughly relishing the anticipated joy awaiting them. Everyone seemed delighted but me; I was all churned up inside.

In my home moral principles had been taught me from my childhood. I knew right from wrong. And I knew stealing was wrong. Even under the guise of a Halloween prank, I could not feel free to steal. Besides this, because my childhood had included active participation in church activities, I also knew the Bible's teachings against the use of alcoholic beverages.

That night in the vacant lot two passages memorized years before from the Scriptures flashed through my mind: "Wine is a mocker, strong drink is raging: and whosoever is deceived thereby is not wise." Proverbs 20:1. "Look not thou upon the wine when it is red, when it giveth his colour in the cup, when it moveth itself aright. At the last it biteth like a serpent, and stingeth like an adder." Proverbs 23:31, 32. I knew these verses were against all alcoholic beverages.

In retrospect I cannot proudly state that I was brave that night in the face of my friends' taunts and ridicule. No well-worded speeches containing factual information on the evils of alcohol came from me. As a matter of fact, what I really remember is being pretty uncomfortable and more than a bit humiliated at being the object of their unrelenting scorn. But I did turn down their invitation to join them in drinking that night, as I have done all the years of my life since. What is more, I have never regretted it, not for a single instant.

That night two of those boys started down a new road for them, which has been a serious problem in their lives ever since. For one of them the problem has been so serious that it is probably safe to say that alcohol has ruined his life. Their ridicule was hard for me to take then, but today I am glad that I did. Now they are enslaved by a costly and ruinous habit. I have often wondered if they ever think of that Halloween night more than thirty years ago. And if so, maybe their teen-age scorn has given way to middle-age envy.

The passing years have brought me into contact on more than one occasion with the growing and deeply perplexing problem of alcoholism in human lives. Mary, a member of my congregation, was one of the finest, most cultured, and gentle ladies I have ever met. She was a real aristocrat of the old school. Charles, her husband, not a church member, was equally polished. He was educated, refined, dignified, and commanding in appearance. Anyone would have taken him for a successful business executive, which he had once been.

One night, soon after I had moved to the parish where they lived, I received a call from Mary asking me to come to their home immediately. I was quite unprepared for what I found in their humble little apartment. Charles was sitting at the kitchen table hopelessly intoxicated, and, unfortunately, he continued drinking. That night I found that their home was humble because practically everything of value had been pawned to secure money to feed that insatiable thirst.

His wife wanted me to come and say the magic words which would make him stop drinking, for she had learned through bitter experience to fear him when he was under the influence of alcohol. He became almost a maniac.

But I had no easy solution then, nor have I found any since. One feels helpless in attempting to reason with a man whose reasoning ability is seriously curtailed and perhaps temporarily nonexistent. I failed miserably in bettering the immediate situation and left them, but only after the wife had felt it necessary to telephone the police for protection and poor Charles was being hustled off.

Subsequently, I visited by the hour, under all sorts of circumstances, with that unfortunate man—in jail, in the prison ward, and in private rooms of hospitals; at his own kitchen table when he was sober, and at his own kitchen table as he poured drink after drink and downed them quickly; in my own study at the church, and often over the telephone. Infrequently he attended church to the evident delight of his wife, and it was always a pleasure for me to see him there.

When he was himself, he was one of the most considerate men alive; but when alcohol took over, he was changed completely. He tried many things to help him overcome his difficulty —frequent medical treatment, long periods in the hospital "drying out," Alcoholics Anonymous, and to some degree the church. But he always gave up with all of these too soon, for it was evident that he never really wanted strongly enough to be free from drink to stay with anything that could help him. One sad day his heartbroken wife told me that Charles was dead, adding that perhaps this was the only way that he could find freedom from his slavery.

Such a story does not need to end that way, in frustration and failure. Some men have found a power in their lives which has enabled them to stand up against the pressures of society and never begin the practices which would lead to such complete enslavement.

Every Sunday evening for seven years in my New York City pastorate, I conducted religious meetings for the general public in Brooklyn's Academy of Music. As a result of those public meetings, over the intervening years several hundred people began to attend our weekly church services and ultimately became church members. Before baptizing these new members, however, I always made it a point to become personally acquainted with them as far as possible.

I shall never forget one man who desired church membership. At first he seemed deliberately anxious not to talk about himself and would avoid answering any question regarding his family. He gave me a business address rather than his home address. I wondered what he was trying to hide, and I even came to question the genuineness of his desire to be a dedicated and committed part of the church. But one day in a visit with him in the church study, the floodgates burst, and he talked. After that I understood.

He had been an outstanding realtor, but his business had all but disintegrated because of his alcoholism. He had reached the bottom of the ladder.

One night he had wandered into one of our meetings in his desperation and while there obtained a glimmer of hope regarding what God could do for him. He decided to give it a try, and, without discussing it with anyone, he had committed his all to the service of his Maker and had prayed for sustaining grace in order that he might overcome. He had found the help he sought, as does every honest-hearted seeker.

I became convinced that he sincerely meant business, and a few weeks later I baptized him. The subsequent years proved that his experience was genuine, for he never slipped back into the old ways. Ultimately his wife, impressed by the change which had taken place, joined him in the church. Some years later he died, beloved by and enjoying the confidence of everyone.

Why had the one man so gloriously succeeded, when at the same time in the same city and under the influence of the same church the other had so completely failed? The answer is clear. The one had found an experience which the other had failed to grasp. The Bible thus clearly expresses it: "But as many as received him, to them gave he power to become the sons of God, even to them that believe on his name." John 1:12. Many have found that religious faith does indeed bring restoring and sustaining power. They have proved the truth of the Biblical assertion that God "is able to keep you from falling." (Jude 24.)

How does a conversion experience help? Conversion is a miracle of God's grace. It changes men completely. The Bible makes this claim for it: "Therefore if any man be in Christ, he is a new creature: old things are passed away; behold, all things are become new." 2 Corinthians 5:17. While I cannot explain the miraculous change that takes place in the human heart, I know its reality.

The changed outlook which accompanies the finding of a religious experience eliminates the need for escape through alcohol by providing a daily solution to life's problems. When a man can take his problems to God in prayer and leave them there, knowing that a greater power has taken over, he can face his future with a confidence that removes life-shattering fears and the need for the dulling power of alcohol. The need to run away is gone.

Not many weeks ago in a rather dismal room in a poorer section of town, I visited for some time with four narcotics addicts. I would like to call them former addicts, but they would object to that. They are not taking drugs now, but they never want to become overly confident and let down their guard. They will always consider themselves drug addicts and recognize the possibility of slipping back.

One of these individuals had taken drugs steadily for nineteen years, the others for twelve, nine, and seven years. Fewer than 1 percent of addicts become permanently free!

The secret? Each talked earnestly of an experience he had come to call his own "spiritual awakening." At my request, each told me his own story, a story of repeated attempts to "kick the habit," always followed by failure. But now it was different.

Let me emphasize, this thing is real. A vital religious experience provides *preventive power*. I discovered it one Halloween night in my teens. Many a young person has discovered it since under differing circumstances.

12

Religious faith also has *saving power,* which alcoholics, narcotics addicts, and others with various problems of life have discovered.

And its *keeping power* can sustain you and "present you faultless," one day at a time, if you accept it into your life. With all the conviction born of the experiences which have come to me, I heartily recommend to you the power of a vital religious experience.

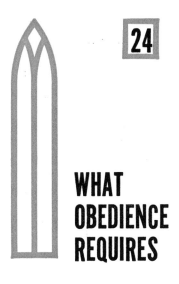

24

WHAT OBEDIENCE REQUIRES

I WAS somewhere on an almost trackless desert area, perhaps midway between the Red Sea and my goal—Mount Sinai. The previous night had been spent in traveling by car from Cairo, Egypt, to Suez so as to arrive at the Canal just before dawn. Once the great ships started to go through at daybreak, the little ferryboat on which we must make the crossing would no longer be allowed to operate. We had just made it. As we traveled in that little vessel across the narrow waterway which separates Africa from Asia, we saw the lights of the day's first ship as it made its way out of the Red Sea and into the Suez Canal. Ours would be the last crossing for many hours.

After crossing the Suez, our rather antiquated taxi—with its quiet and dependable Greek owner, Johnny, at the wheel—started down the shore of the Red Sea on a poor dirt road. For the long journey we had gasoline in large tins on the car's roof, and food enough for three days. We knew that while traveling in this rugged country we were to be pretty much on our own.

Soon Johnny headed away from the sea, and after that there was no road. Contemplating this new situation, I finally cautiously asked the driver how he knew where he was going. He threw his head back and laughed joyously, evidently delighted at my question, and then replied, "Johnny makes his own roads."

And so he did, as I bounced up and down and from side to side in the rear seat, hoping fervently that the squeaking, creaking car would not burn out a clutch or a bearing, or fall apart, or become a victim of any one of a dozen other dreadful catastrophes that my fertile imagination conjured up to plague me. I still think it might have been serious to be stranded out there alone with no villages, no people (except a few wandering Bedouins), and no communication with the outside world.

The more I thought about the isolation, the more I wondered. I even pondered what might happen if my appendix, which incidentally had never given me a moment's trouble or concern, should suddenly flare up. The unhappy conclusion to which I came made me groan in self-pity. With such dark thoughts keeping me constant company, I will probably be remembered best by Johnny and the monks at the abbey at the foot of Mount Sinai for making the fastest trip, turnaround, and return on record! But when on the way back we broke a spring and had to cripple on to civilization, I felt my fears had not been entirely groundless.

Despite my evident concern, however, I was excited and delighted to be making this journey, for I was traveling the very route which the children of Israel covered when they escaped from Egyptian bondage and journeyed to Sinai. Before reaching the majestic mountain from which God thundered the Ten Commandments to Israel, we pulled up before a big, rugged, reddish-brown rock, and Johnny stopped the car. As I got out, he explained tersely that this was the rock which Moses had struck and from which water had gushed forth in that desert area to care for the physical needs of the thousands of Israelites traveling through the place.

While Johnny busied himself adjusting the ropes and straps holding the gasoline tins on the car roof, I stood reflecting. This rock reminded me of another rock, a similar rock—the one to which God had commanded Moses to *speak,* and water would flow forth. But Moses had disobeyed and had *struck* the rock instead. Water gushed forth as promised. But because Moses had substituted something which he considered just as good for a command of God, he sacrificed the privilege of going over into the Promised Land.

The warm sun shone down from a clear, cloudless sky as I pondered why God would be seemingly so exacting. Did it really matter? *Speak* or *strike*—what is the real difference? In either case it would take a miracle from God to provide the water. No matter what other reasons may have existed for God's expressed displeasure over Moses' deed, I am sure that one of the main reasons was His desire to indicate to all the people of Israel and, for that matter, to all of us who follow after, that He *is* particular. When He commands us to speak, we are not to strike. In other words, we are never, never to substitute our way for God's, our plans for His, something "just as good" for what He has requested.

If you will give the matter even a little thought, you will doubtless realize that God has shown again and again in His Word that He is particular about how we obey Him. On a variety of occasions He has demonstrated unmistakably that it does matter to Him whether or not we are obedient. As a matter of fact, that truth was revealed soon after the dawn of human history, when Cain and Abel first offered sacrifices. God had asked that a lamb be slain in connection with securing Heaven's forgiveness for sins. This lamb was to prefigure Jesus, the Lamb of God who would die to take away the sins of the world.

But Cain did not think what he offered really mattered. It was the principle of the thing, he reasoned, and not the minute details. The idea was that everyone was to sacrifice—it did not really matter how or what. And so he offered some of his fruits and vegetables instead of the requested lamb. "And the Lord had respect unto Abel and to his offering: but unto Cain and to his offering he had not respect." Genesis 4:4, 5. To his sorrow Cain found that it did matter. Taking out on his brother his frustration at being rejected by God, Cain committed the very first murder of all history. It was savage and unprovoked. To the end of his troubled days he bore a mark to remind him that with God details *do* matter.

Many people today are making the same mistake made by Moses and Cain. Are you by chance one of them? For instance, God's Word is unmistakable in enjoining the observance of the seventh-day Sabbath; but many feel that as long as they keep one day out of the seven, it will be all right with God. "After all, what's the difference," they ask, "if you speak or strike, if you bring lambs or grapes? It's the big, broad principles that count, not the minute details. Saturday or Sunday, or even Friday," they say—"I could not care less, and surely it doesn't matter with God." But do not the lessons of the past mean anything to such individuals? If they do—and I surely believe they should—then it *does* make a difference; it *does* matter.

The beliefs and actions of some individuals indicate that they feel the fourth commandment should read, "a seventh part of time is the sabbath," and "Remember the sabbath institution, to keep it holy." But the Bible does not say that. Instead it very specifically states, "The seventh *day* is the sabbath," and "Remember the sabbath *day,* to keep it holy." Some would perhaps like the commandment to read, "But the seventh day is the sabbath of the Jews"; but instead it reads, "The seventh day is the *sabbath of the Lord thy God:* in it thou shalt not do any work." Dare we trifle with anything as explicit as this, especially when we know that with God it *does* matter?

The New Testament points out how particular God is in regard to the keeping of His commandments. To the commandment which prohibits murder the Apostle John added, "Whosoever hateth his brother is a murderer." 1 John 3:15. Regarding the commandment prohibiting unfaithfulness to marriage vows Jesus' comment was, "Whosoever looketh on a woman to lust after her hath committed adultery with her already in his heart."

Matthew 5:28. This shows how particular God is about these commandments. Of equal importance is the keeping of God's wonderful Sabbath day, which is a special gift to us from our Creator.

Any who feel that they can honor God better through a substitution of their own plans for God's should remember an experience which came to Israel. God had commanded Saul to go out and utterly destroy Amalek (1 Samuel 15:3), but Saul could not quite bring himself to do it, and he saved some of the best of the sheep and oxen. When Samuel the prophet discovered what had been done, Saul explained that these animals were to be sacrificed to the Lord. The prophet replied with a great and eternal truth: "To obey is better than sacrifice, and to hearken than the fat of rams." Verse 22. All the sacrifices in the world, including substantial gifts to God's work and extensive time devoted to church enterprises, will not atone for a lack of obedience. Never forget it. It *does* matter.

We Christians are dependent upon the finished work of Christ on Calvary to bring us salvation from sin and a place in God's kingdom. Did you ever realize that according to the Scriptures Christ "became the author of eternal salvation unto all them that obey him"? (Hebrews 5:9.) These words definitely imply that a lack of obedience may be equated with a rejection of Jesus Christ as our Saviour from sin. Such a situation leaves no room for doubt that it is important that we obey.

Christ Himself declared, "Not every one that saith unto me, Lord, Lord, shall enter into the kingdom of heaven; but he that doeth the will of my Father which is in heaven." Matthew 7:21. Jesus, when asked by a certain man, "Good Master, what good thing shall I do, that I may have eternal life?" replied, "If thou wilt enter into life, keep the commandments." Matthew 19:16, 17. Then Jesus made it clear that He was talking about the Ten Commandments by quoting some of them. The plain and unequivocal truth is that Jesus never came to save anyone *in* disobedience. He came rather to save us *from* our disobedience, to free us from our past sins and mistakes, and to give us power and grace to live for Him from day to day.

When Jesus lived in this world, His nation had amassed a great deal of human tradition around the law of God. Christ rebuked the scribes, Pharisees, and religious leaders for this. Searchingly He asked, "Why do ye also transgress the commandment of God by your tradition?" Then He added, almost in exasperation, "In vain they do worship me, teaching for doctrines the commandments of men." Matthew 15:3, 9. If Christ were living among men today, I wonder what He would say regarding the human tradition that has taken the place of commands of God.

Without wanting to belabor the point, may I remind you that the observance of the first day of the week, so universally accepted in Christendom today, stands upon nothing more solid than the perishable foundation of human tradition. Men have truly substituted their own traditions for the commandments of God once again. Christ's words on this matter have application to our present day. He calls any worship based on the traditions of men a "vain" worship. We too should recognize it as such and spurn it.

When Jesus comes to earth the second time, to receive a people to Himself, of whom will He take special note? This is what we are told by John the revelator: "Here is the patience of the saints: here are they that keep the commandments of God, and the faith of Jesus." Revelation 14:12. A faithful observance of God's commandments and a victorious witness to faith in the Lord Jesus Christ—these two characteristics will be found hand in hand in the people who are preparing to meet Jesus Christ and are receiving His approval.

Let us never think that any command of the Almighty does not matter. He who sees to it that the stars in heaven all follow dependently and without deviation their appointed courses, operates His whole universe in just that way. Do not try to substitute. Obey. Do not reason that something else is just as good. It is not.

Do not teach "for doctrines the commandments of men." They are not adequate. Always remember: With God it *does* matter.

We who are parents look for obedience in our children as evidence of their love for us. The Lord of glory wants us, His children, to show our love for Him in the same way: "If ye love me," He pleads, "keep my commandments." John 14:15.

David the psalmist expresses his devotion in the words, "I delight to do thy will, O my God: yea, thy law is within my heart." Psalm 40:8. This should be the sentiment of all of us. I repeat it again at this moment, placing my life upon God's altar for obedient service, thus accepting Christ anew as the Author of my salvation. Will you join me? Remember, it *does* matter.

25

DESTINATION: ETERNITY

THE WEATHER was cold and blustery on New York's lower Broadway on March 1, 1962. The air was already filled with tons of ticker tape and confetti, kept aloft by the brisk wind. Even though the pressing crowd about me had pinned my arms to my sides, I managed to get my watch up to where I could see it. In fifteen more minutes John Glenn would arrive to receive a hero's welcome such as the country had never seen before. He would be accompanied by his family, by the Vice-president of the United States, and by America's other astronauts. I was glad I was there to participate.

And they were on time! Just before noon, preceded by bands representing all the armed services, the car bearing the Glenns and the Vice-president arrived. The multitudes lining the street literally went wild as they shouted their acclaim. And then for my particular block it was over, and he was borne in triumph on up Broadway. Later I realized that I had not even noticed the Vice-president and had scarcely seen Mrs. Glenn. Like everyone else that day, my eyes had been on the hero.

What had produced all this adulation which caught up even the most sophisticated in its swelling tide? Everyone knows that a few days before, this man had soared into outer space and orbited the earth three times—the first man from the free world, at least, ever to do so. When he left on his journey through space, he could not be absolutely sure he would ever come back to earth alive again. Any number of malfunctions could have snuffed out his life. The nation, and in fact most of the world, had been awed by his courage and daring and thrilled by his successful return. I felt that day that he deserved every bit of the gratitude and spontaneous acclaim which he was receiving. In every sense he had pioneered in a new and devastatingly dangerous field and had come back safely.

After he had passed, I made my way down a side street and returned to my office, lost in thought about it all. A new door was now open, a new and endless ocean had been revealed, and men were beginning to sail its uncharted vastnesses. There will be others, I thought, and others and others, until the whole thing perhaps will become commonplace. But then another, even more startling, thought came to me, a thought which persisted as I continued down the street: *I too will soon travel in space*—and not in a space capsule fired by a mighty rocket, either. I am making preparations every day for the journey.

As I walked out of the cold wind and down into a subway station, my mind repeated the words of a familiar scripture: "Then we . . . shall be caught up . . . in the clouds." Those few words foretell the space travel in which I plan soon to participate. In fact, everyone who really wants to can participate in it, and one of the reassuring wonders of it all is that it is absolutely and completely safe. Here is the entire promise of the scripture of which my "space travel" words form a part:

"For the Lord himself shall descend from heaven with a shout, with the voice of the archangel, and with the trump of God: and the dead in Christ shall rise first: then we which are alive and remain shall be caught up together with them in the clouds, to meet the Lord in the air: and so shall we ever be with the Lord." 1 Thessalonians 4:16, 17.

The prophet Job spoke of this experience in these words: "In my flesh shall I see God." Job 19:26. Therefore I do not hesitate to admit that I am looking forward with the greatest of expectations to my flesh-and-blood experience as an astronaut.

A few years ago it sounded fantastic for anyone to speak of an approaching time when man would be able to travel at speeds exceeding 17,000 miles an hour and at heights of more than one hundred miles, orbiting the earth three times in little more than four hours. I can hardly believe even now that it has been done and that space flights since have so greatly exceeded it. Therefore I suppose there are some who will find it difficult to believe that an event such as the Scriptures describe could ever take place. But after what our eyes have seen, how can we in all fairness disbelieve?

The Bible states that the Lord Jesus Christ will descend from heaven and awaken the dead. Then the righteous, both the resurrected ones and those alive when the Lord comes, will be caught up together in the clouds to meet Him in the air, thus starting upon the greatest space journey of all time. And after that, our Lord promises, we are to be forever with Him.

A very real purpose is planned for this venture into space described in the Bible. It is not to be an aimless wandering in orbit for the sake of conquering space or time; rather, these events will be a part of the keeping of a great promise given by God to man centuries ago. This promise was repeated and verified by Jesus when He was here on earth. It is referred to more times in the New Testament than any other single subject. The promise has to do with the second advent of the Lord, at which time the space trip for the saved of earth will take place. Here is the promise, in John 14:1-3, just as it came from the lips of Jesus:

"Let not your heart be troubled: ye believe in God, believe also in me. In my Father's house are many mansions: if it were not so, I would have told you. I go to prepare a place for you. And if I go and prepare a place for you, I will come again, and receive you unto myself; that where I am, there ye may be also."

The promise was repeated to the disciples under unusual circumstances by angels from heaven at the time of Christ's ascension. "And while they looked stedfastly toward heaven as he went up, behold, two men stood by them in white apparel; which also said, Ye men of Galilee, why stand ye gazing up into heaven? this same Jesus, which is taken up from you into heaven, shall so come in like manner as ye have seen him go into heaven." Acts 1:10, 11.

But the promise was given through the inspiration of the prophets much earlier than this. "And Enoch also, the seventh from Adam, prophesied of these, saying, Behold, the Lord cometh with ten thousands of his saints." Jude 14.

Over and over again the promise is repeated in the Scriptures. Job spoke of it (Job 19:25-27); David referred to it (Psalms 50: 3; 96:13); Peter affirmed that "we have not followed cunningly devised fables, when we made known unto you the power and coming of our Lord Jesus Christ" (2 Peter 1:16); Paul called it "that blessed hope" (Titus 2:13). Yet many seem to know very little about Christ's second coming, and relatively few sermons are preached on it. Why?

Dwight L. Moody, the great nineteenth-century preacher, suggested an answer which is perhaps as good as any: "To my mind this precious doctrine—for such I must call it—of the return of the Lord to this earth is taught in the New Testament as clearly as any other doctrine in it. . . .

"Yet I was in the Church fifteen or sixteen years before I ever heard a sermon on it. There is hardly any church that does not make a great deal of baptism, but in all of Paul's epistles I believe baptism is spoken of only thirteen times, while he speaks about the return of our Lord fifty times; and yet the Church has had very little to say about it. Now, I can see a reason for this; *the devil does not want us to see this truth,* for nothing would wake up the Church so much. The moment a man realizes that Jesus Christ is coming back again to receive His followers to Himself, this world loses its hold upon him. Gas stocks and water stocks and stocks in banks and railroads are of very much less consequence to him then. His heart is free, and he looks for the blessed appearing of his Lord, who, at His coming, will take him into His blessed Kingdom."—*The Second Coming of Christ*, pp. 6, 7.

A belief so important should have a prominent place in our lives. As a matter of fact, the last book of the Bible, the Book of Revelation, sets an example for us. This postascension gospel (for such it is) was inspired and written fifty years after Jesus had returned to heaven. One of the first things said in Revelation is, "Behold, he cometh with clouds; and every eye shall see him." Revelation 1:7. And one of the last things written is, "Surely I come quickly." Revelation 22:20. The "blessed hope" is referred to all through the book, showing what our Saviour had in mind as He sent this message back to earth. Should not the second coming occupy an equally prominent place in all our thinking, planning, and conversation?

Our future journey into space is to take us home to be with Jesus and the saved of earth forever. It is to reunite us with our dear ones who have been claimed by death. It is to give us the long-promised eternal life and do away with sin and its effects forever. It will be the happiest journey of all time, for it will truly be the "journey into tomorrow," the trip which can entirely qualify as our own personal "dream trip," the journey which will make dreams come true.

Years of preparation preceded John Glenn's orbital flight into space—the preparations of the booster, the capsule, the various guidance systems; the plans for reentry and ultimate recovery. And not the least of all was the preparation of John Glenn himself. For several years he had spared nothing in preparing himself for this big day, his great opportunity. He had groomed himself physically by running five miles each day and engaging in other taxing physical activities calculated to give him a strong body capable of maximum resistance to unusual situations and pressures.

Mental preparations were also needed to equip him adequately for the new and untried conditions he would meet in outer space, teaching him how to cope with the various problems which would arise. Emotional preparations were needed, preconditioning him for hours of isolation in an incredibly small space as he would endure weightlessness, heat, cold, brilliant sunlight, darkness, and short days and nights in an entirely new and different world. For years he had bent every energy with single-minded purpose into ultimately riding the space capsule around the earth. As he looks back, he feels that it was worth it all.

With a much greater prize at stake, can we do less? Should we be surprised if our journey into space calls for some preparation also? Could we possibly make it were we not prepared?

Our preparation for this space journey is, first of all, spiritual. It includes an acceptance of Jesus Christ as our personal Saviour, a recognition that His blood shed on Calvary pays the price for sin. It includes asking God for a new heart with changed and renewed desires, motives, and affections. It includes a turning away from every known sin and a positive turning to righteousness, or right living. It includes an old-fashioned experience which our fathers called "conversion"—a right-about-face, a U turn on the highway of life.

Thus the preparation for our great space flight includes the laying aside of some things which would certainly get in the way. "Every man that hath this hope in him purifieth himself, even as he is pure." 1 John 3:3. Let Jesus explain it in His own words: "Take heed to yourselves, lest at any time your hearts be overcharged with surfeiting, and drunkenness, and cares of this life, and so that day come upon you unawares. . . . Watch ye therefore, and pray always, that ye may be accounted worthy to escape all these things that shall come to pass, and to stand before the Son of man." Luke 21:34-36.

Here is the counsel which James gives to us: "Be patient therefore, brethren, unto the coming of the Lord. Behold, the husbandman waiteth for the precious fruit of the earth, and hath long patience for it, until he receive the early and latter rain. Be ye also patient; stablish your hearts: for the coming of the Lord draweth nigh." James 5:7, 8.

Yes, soon I too shall travel in space! To the moon? Perhaps. To far-off stars and planets? It is possible. But most important, I will go to my heavenly home, and Jesus, my Saviour, will triumphantly lead the way. He will forever do away with sin, sickness, death, pain, and separation.

I look forward to my space journey with Him. Because I have accepted His sacrifice on Calvary for my sins, I can say confidently with Paul, "Henceforth there is laid up for me a crown of righteousness, which the Lord, the righteous judge, shall give me at that day: and not to me only, but unto all them also that love his appearing." 2 Timothy 4:8.

Can you say this, too?

Start Feb 10/67 — Feb 22/67.